My Steamboat

A Ski Town Childhood

DORI DECAMILLIS

10/12

Library of Congress Number: 2009909765
ISBN#: 1-4392-5937-2

Front and Back Cover Photos: Buddy Bair

Published by
Double You Zee Press

To Mom, Dad, Debi, Derick, Dana and Granny, and to the loving memory of Tom Duckels, Francis Staub, and Patsy Wilhelm.

Introduction

The history of Steamboat Springs, Colorado overflows with tales of courageous settlers, proud Native Americans, rowdy cowboys, famous bull-riders, enterprising developers, and legendary Olympic skiers. Not mentioned in the chronicles of this small town are the ordinary people who earned a living at regular jobs, fished the rivers, skied with average skill, married and raised families, attended church and school, bore the deep snow and bitter cold every winter, and worshipped summer as if it would never come again. Although some might not call my family common, we were part of the everyday population.

I didn't realize in my younger days that I was watching our rural, ranching and mining town turn into a world-class ski resort. I couldn't appreciate at the time the interesting interplay between two enormously different cultures trying to make or keep the town the way they wanted it. I heard tourists making fun of the local hicks (namely me) on rare occasions, but more frequently I witnessed natives bashing the "turkeys," our nickname for tourists. In the 70's, when the ski resort was owned by some wealthy Texans, someone stamped a message into the snow on a hill near the ski area that read, "If God wanted Texans to ski He would have made bullshit white." But for the most part the two factions seemed to adapt to each other because they had to, with relatively little confrontation. The tourists needed someone to wait on them. And it was impossible for natives to deny that, along with their ridiculous outfits and flashy manners, newcomers and visitors brought something supremely important: money.

As one of the native residents I watched the affluent vacationers, freewheeling ski bums, transient hippies, and citified new inhabitants with mixed emotions. Like all the locals I yelled at them for their inferior snow-driving skills, even before I could drive. I sometimes hated that they thought they owned the place, but I was jealous of their (sometimes) fashionable clothes and progressive attitudes. I looked with wonder at automobile license plates from all the over the country and got good at guessing which type of people came from where. I had fun boasting with my friends on the ski bus or ski lifts about being a real native, trying to get the turkeys to envy us. (I'm pretty sure they did.)

Eventually I got used to the swollen population in winter and the changing face of the town. Seeing all sorts of people from all over the globe on our streets and in our restaurants became commonplace. The outsiders blended in with the scenery (as much as could be expected) and we indigenous folks were generally more comfortable keeping to ourselves. Many of us found security in sticking to our old ways, and it's possible we held more tightly to our ideals and habits as a reaction to the constant barrage of newfangled everything. It is likely that my family responded to this enforced blending by becoming more wedded to our eccentricities.

True to my parents' peculiarity, they named their children (going from oldest to youngest) Dori, Debi, Derick, and Dana. Our last name is Duckels. My mom's tongue was perpetually twisted, and we all endured a lifetime of uninterrupted teasing. By the time I reached college I'd heard every derivative and rhyme of the word DUCK humans could possibly come up with. I was always astounded at how funny and original a new acquaintance thought they were when calling me Quackles or Ducky. Boy, that's a new one, I'd say for the nine-thousandth time. The amount of teasing I received in Steamboat may have been slightly less than what I would have endured in other places, though, as we had an inordinate amount of people with weird names. Growing up with Barbie Bacon, Gretchen Yechenbacher, Katie Krautkramer, Bill Buckles, Rowdy Raspberry (on his birth certificate), Pam Pitts, Gordon Guzzle, Buddy Bair (who shot the photograph for the cover of this book) Casey Clapsaddle, Duncan Craighead, Rims Hiney, Rex Peelstix, and Dewey Whitecotton took some of the pressure off the D. Duckels.

My story takes place in the 1960s and 70s, when Steamboat people did not lock the doors of their cars or homes, and hitchhiking was a standard form of transportation. To get to destinations around town or out to the ski mountain, grandmothers and children hitchhiked as often as twenty-something men with long beards. Children were perfectly safe exploring miles from home—whether around town, into the fields of nearby ranches, or out into the surrounding wilderness. The influx of strangers from the city didn't seem to change the sense of safety and trust.

Perhaps Steamboat was too remote, humble, and cold for robbers and rapists to make the trip.

The world today might be somewhat unsympathetic to what we found funny and acceptable back then. Steamboat natives were toughened by weather and isolation. Too busy battling the elements, living everyday life, and finding fun without electronic media, we tended to see political correctness and citified gentilities as unsavory or worse—a waste of time. My apologies to my modern readers who find us uncivilized. I grew up thinking everything we did was completely normal.

When Cats Fly

In the fall of 1963, in a small red and white trailer at Dream Island Trailer Park, Mom and Dad had three babies: me, Wooch and Priscilla. Wooch was a Collie puppy, already smart and obedient at the age of a few weeks. Even as a kitten Priscilla was a grumpy, longhaired gray Persian with little patience for me. And I was a human baby.

Dream Island was and still is neither dreamy nor an island. A thin strip of land between Highway 40 and the Yampa River, just past the park with the Sulphur Spring, its two rows of scruffy trailers marked the end of town back then. My parents moved there when they were first married because it was all they could afford, but were grateful to move out a year later to a real house over on Spruce Street, in the middle of town. I remember nothing of life in the trailer, but black and white photos bordered in white show me in my jammies flanked by Wooch and Pricilla, or me being held up by my Dad while Wooch pokes her head in the picture.

Neither of my parents remembers how they obtained their first dog and cat, but rest assured they paid nothing for them. Except for their lifetimes of one-a-day servings of dry generic food, almost never would a Duckels animal cost us a cent, be it for acquiring them or maintaining their health. Perhaps through animal intuition our pets knew they must remain healthy or die and thus lived longer than most pets without ever getting sick or being given a bath. My parents' apparent neglect of their animals was not uncommon in Steamboat in those days. Most of our friends lived on farms and ranches where dogs and cats are treated with less care than livestock. A horse caught in barbed wire or a cow with birthing trouble would require the services of Pinky Smith, the vet. But in our circle of friends I don't recall a dog or cat seeing Pinky. A rock or gunshot to the head was the answer to anything that couldn't be cured by nature. And nature almost always did the trick.

Wooch, our Collie, was a special animal, our most special ever. As smart as Lassie (or so we thought) and just as beautiful, she did tricks and played fetch and let us dress her up and did exactly as she was told. After Mom made a harness for her to pull our little red wagon in the summer, Wooch would follow behind Mom, pulling my sister Debi and me to various errands around town. In winter she was hitched to a radio flyer sled. Following my fast-walking mother and toting us kids bundled like Eskimos she glided through the streets of Steamboat to the amusement and adoration of most who saw us. We knew of no other mothers who carted their kids through town behind a sled dog. Once we got our picture in the *Steamboat Pilot*, the town paper, as we rolled in the wagon down the newly thawed sidewalks of Main Street. A woman came running out of the Pilot Office Supply with her camera in hand, asking for our photograph.

"What a stupid thing to take a picture of," I thought. "We're just going around getting stuff."

Mom straightened up our scarves and hats while the Pilot lady positioned our hands in a wave for the camera.

"No fakey smiles," Mom whispered in our ears.

The large, bold caption below the published photo read, *A Little Red Wagon And A Waggin' Tail.* Our smiles were indeed fakey, and our waves looked posed, but the clipping remains as a testimony to my mother's ingenuity and self-reliance, and to Wooch's goodness.

Throughout our younger years Wooch's nobility contrasted with Priscilla's grouchiness. The old gray cat wanted nothing to do with kids and loved only my mother. Barely a part of our lives, she skulked on the perimeter of our play in the backyard and hissed if we ever came too near. Most of the time she was too ugly to warrant stroking anyway. Like all Duckels animals for all time she was an outdoor-only cat and grew an impenetrably thick coat in winter, able to withstand temperatures far, far below zero. When spring came, her coat shed in bulky, knotty clumps of matted hair that clung to her sides and belly until summer was nearly over. Some of the hair mounds would drag behind her on the ground as she bumbled clumsily along. Friends would ask, "Why don't you cut them off?" Mom had tried that and left Priscilla with long, pink patches of exposed skin mixed with bloody specks and areas of stubborn, still clinging hair tufts. As bad as she looked without trimming she definitely looked worse after Mom got a hold of her. Knowing my mom's hair-butchering techniques for cats, a new-to-Steamboat friend once asked, "Why don't you take her to the vet to be trimmed?" I looked at my friend as if she had just suggested I go bowling with my own head for a ball.

Professional animal grooming was as remote a prospect to our family as buying gold leaf toilet paper.

By October, when Priscilla's hair would finally shed the last of its loathsomeness, winter would come to fluff her up and begin the cycle again. To us, Priscilla's appearance fit her personality.

At eight years old our wonderful Wooch was diagnosed with cancer. It was the only time I remember Pinky the Vet treating one of our animals. Wooch had grown to be much loved, and I guess Mom and Dad couldn't imagine putting her down without seeing if something could be done. A few months after being diagnosed, Wooch's quiet suffering ended. Not long after that, I accidentally watched a television show that helped me dredge up and spill the tears that hadn't come since her death. The bedroom I shared with Debi was attached to that of my parents, and from the top bunk of our trundle bed I could see into the mirror of my mother's vanity, which reflected perfectly their small black and white TV perched atop a chest of drawers. I didn't mean to become absorbed in the show they were watching. It was some modernized Old Yeller type movie, only sappier. At the end, when the bell-bottomed, big-collared family huddled together, weeping over the loss of their ordinary dog (no where near as good as Wooch) I sobbed uncontrollably, drowning the sounds in my pillow.

I didn't like the hurting or crying one bit. It seemed much smarter to stoically adopt the farmer and rancher approach to dying pets. Most of my friends seem to do fine with this attitude. I made a silent pact with myself to remain unemotional about losing animals, as it would probably happen many times in my life. I never cried about Wooch again, or any other of our dead animals, until I was in college. It was way too painful.

Months after Wooch's death, much to the annoyance of mean Priscilla, a new beautiful cat was given to us by friends—a soft, gray and white, partially striped cat that we called Cedar, named after the wood we were using to build our new house. We kids were enamored of her. Here was a supremely soft cat that loved to be stroked, with hair that never clumped in the springtime. She and Priscilla stayed away from each other unless temperatures became so drastically low as to necessitate a temporary cat truce, at which time the two half-frozen enemies would curl up together in a tight ball underneath the back porch. We rarely came upon them in this compromising position, but if we did the two prideful females would split up hastily and pretend as if they knew nothing of the other strange cat.

I'm still not sure why Mom brought Max home. We were all certain that any dog would pale in the shadow of Wooch. Mom told us one day that she was going to Walden, a small ranching town a few hours a way, to pick up a new dog for us and no, it wasn't a puppy, and no, we couldn't come with her. We listened at home impatiently for the familiar crunching sound of our old Kingswood Estate station wagon pulling into the driveway paved with clinkers from the coal furnace. It was summer.

Finally Mom arrived, yelling obscenities at someone in the back seat, out of our view. She got out, opened the back door, and grabbed by the scruff of the neck a frightened black dog which she tossed out of the car.

"She was supposed to be a regular black lab. This dog is a goddamn pipsqueak. You can hardly tell it's a lab.

And she's afraid of everything. This is all I need." Mom had driven all the way to Walden and learned that our new dog wasn't exactly what the owner had described. The situation called for colorful language.

The four of us ran over to pet the dog, which, eager to soak up our attention, wiggled her rear end with her tail between her legs and her ears back. She *was* a wimp, and she barely looked like a Labrador Retriever, but she was friendly and didn't seem to mind that four strange children were smothering her with affection.

"What's her name?" my brother Derick asked.

Mom was busy hauling groceries out of the car, and muttered over the top of an overflowing bag, "Max. Short for Maxine. Great. We have a goddamn girl dog named Max."

"We could change it," I offered.

"She's too old. You can't change a dog's name when they're this old. Now help me with these goddamn groceries."

While we hauled sacks inside, Debi asked, "Is that all the bigger she's going to get? I thought we were getting a big dog".

"Those assholes never told me she was a runt. She's a runt. That's why she's not big. That's why she doesn't even look like a lab. She'll never get any bigger than this. She'll always be a wimpy—hey! Put those on this counter! This goddamn kitchen is too small..."

We ran outside to play with Max.

Max never got bigger and most of our friends asked what kind of dog she was, even though almost everyone in Steamboat owned a lab. She looked like a pig-dog. She cowered if you said hello to her, never barked, nearly always had her tail between her legs, could do no tricks or games, and obeyed no commands except for "Here Max!" which meant it was time to eat. But she loved us all and stayed in the yard. We often heard Mom wishing aloud that that goddamn dog would run away, but Max never did.

The ultimate proof that Max was not a guard dog came one night when Mom and Dad were eating out at Mazzola's, Steamboat's most popular Italian restaurant at that time. Max was for some reason along for the ride and was left sleeping out in the station wagon while they ate. My parents returned to their car to find Max asleep in the back seat curled up in the arms of a drunken hippie.

The closest Max came to acting like a self-respecting dog was after we'd had her for a few years. Out of the blue she was overtaken by her primal instincts. She would leave each morning for an hour or so and return with one of two mouth-watering items: a big sack of fresh donuts or a wrapped, raw steak. One day steak. The next donuts. Two days in a row steak. Next day donuts. She'd prance nonchalantly into the backyard, methodically dig a deep hole on the side of our yard, drop her prize into it, and cover it back up. We kids tried in vain throughout the daytime to catch Max excavating her feast and devouring it, but she never pulled it out when we were around. Maybe she just left it there. With perfect sincerity I asked Mom why we couldn't take the steak and cook it up, or eat the donuts for breakfast. I received the obvious answers about germs and staleness. I secretly dreamed of eating donuts or steak for breakfast and looked forward each morning to Max's return from her outings when I would lick my chops while watching out the kitchen window, vicariously living through our dog. Max's ritual lasted about a month until we reluctantly tied her up to prevent her from continuing. We loved the fact that Max was doing something special, something that required instinct and intelligence and guts, but we knew she must be committing doggie-robbery. We felt guilty about the human victims who probably missed their meat and sugar. We never found out where the food came from. And I missed my imaginary breakfasts.

I was ten when we moved to "the new house" up Fish Creek Road. By then our pet collection had grown to include two more cats, Raisin and Herman. Any visitor to the Duckels home was always astounded at the welcome they were given. No humans came out to greet them—we Duckels were never known for our social skills—but our pets exemplified the pinnacle of hospitality. A visitor would exit his or her vehicle (usually a pick-up in Steamboat) and Max would creep up sheepishly with a wagging rear-end while the cats would come running from every direction, meowing loudly. Raisin would stand on her hind legs and arch her back to beg for a petting while Cedar and Herman would lean against the person's legs, rubbing their ears on the guest's pants and wrapping their tails around the now unbalanced visitor's ankles. We heard more than a few times from our visitors that our pets were so friendly it was scary.

Our new home was situated at the end of Huckleberry Lane, an incredibly private location. If you walked straight out our front door and kept going, you could walk through hundreds of miles of wilderness. We never determined what city in Wyoming you'd eventually run into, but we fantasized, not unrealistically, that you would probably miss any sign of human life at all until you reached the Canadian Border, three states away. We owned four acres of sagebrush and Aspen groves with a clear view from our picture window of Steamboat, the ski mountain, the Yampa Valley, and all the way out to the Flattops, a spectacular wilderness area nearly 50 miles away.

Living in the country presented the perfect conditions for another pet, one Mom had wanted since girlhood—a horse. The Duckels' No-Cost-Pet-Rule applied even to large animals so we waited until our rancher friends, the Wilhelms, needed to get rid of one.

Casey was big, black, and very old.

Patsy Wilhelm wasn't sure of his age, but thought 17 or 18 was a good guess. Mom was convinced when we got him home that he was 25. He had a fat belly, and his swayback was nearly 17 hands tall. Mom figured he'd be gentle with us kids because he was so worn out. She was right. But Casey was smart and stubborn, too. He rightfully believed he was too old to be carting kids around and continually expressed his wish to be put out to pasture by stretching to eat grass no matter who was riding him or when. It took strong arms to keep his head up and the little kids had no luck in getting him to go anywhere except to the side of the road to graze. I was as rough on Casey as Mom was on the cats, and it took just that kind of doggedness to keep him in line.

When we first got Casey, each morning we'd let him out of his corral to wander. He'd run over the mountains back to his former home at the Wilhelm's. They lived in Elk River Estates—clear through town and 15 miles out. We had no fenced pasture, so Dad devised a "ball and chain" for Casey, out of a leather ankle strap, a super thick chain, and a giant bulldozer wheel drum. Casey towed the weight around our land all day, while he ate non-stop like a lawn-mowing sheep. The wheel drum crushed grass, sage and skunk cabbage and marred the trunks of our aspens. Three or four times a day Mom would yell, "Somebody go unhook Casey," after he'd get his chain wrapped around an aspen so many times he'd be inches from the tree. Without grass within reach and chained to the tree he'd have nothing to do but stare into space or fall asleep until someone released him.

Casey's back leg became conditioned to the load, and his grazing area became larger. In the evenings when time came to put him in his corral for the night we'd search longer and harder for him, and eventually he was able to drag his wheel completely over the first mountain behind our house. Once he was found, the poor kid whose job it was to retrieve him had to lead him home at the pace it took an 18-year-old horse to drag a bulldozer wheel over a mountain. Not fast. We never got home before dark, and although we bragged about how strong our horse was, we always complained about the job.

Every spring Raisin and Cedar would have kittens. This meant we kids had at least 10 kittens to give away each year. After our pet population reached six, Mom assured us no more were staying with us. She'd drop us off at Safeway or City Market (which were just across Main Street from each other) and say, "Give them away or I'll put them to sleep." We knew she'd never pay a vet to kill them, that the kittens' lives would come to a much more gruesome end, so we tried extra hard to make sure they got homes before the end of the weekend. They always did. No one ever asked why we didn't get the cats fixed. It wasn't uncommon to let cats keep producing. Farmers could always use a few extra mice-chasers. It wasn't like the big city where alley cats could multiply and take over. It was too damn cold.

When Dana was little we never had a hard time pushing cats off on people. Her cute little button nose combined with those precious little kitties always sucked in the bleeding hearts. With all four of us skinny kids telling how we couldn't go home until the cats were gone, only the most callous individual could resist—or those who would be at Safeway or City Market the next week with *their* litter. Cat-pushing became more difficult as we aged, and longer hours and more desperate tactics were necessary to dump our load, but we always delivered. No cats were going to be exterminated on our watch.

The years passed.

Raisin, a longhair cat, had the same bad hair affliction that Grumpy Priscilla had been cursed with, but she was so lovable that we scratched around her clumps anyway. She was nuts about love. She'd give up food or sleep to be close to a person. She was so eager to be stroked, even by strangers, her eyes would bug out. When someone walked out a door she'd dart over and allow herself to be trampled just so someone would notice her and bend down to pet her. It was hard not to like her. It was impossible, actually. If we were in bad moods we knew there was always one being in the world that would smother us with adoration and consolation as long as we needed it. She never tired of giving.

Herman would take summer vacations, for months at a time. He'd leave when the leaves had turned completely green—not early at 7,000 ft. elevation—and come back when the aspens first started to show yellow. He lived off the land, we are sure, because he was an excellent hunter. He'd often catch speedy chipmunks and swallow them whole.

Fluffy Cedar remained beautiful until one extremely cold winter night when she crawled up into the car engine to try to stay warm. Fast asleep, she must not have heard Mom get into the car the next morning. Like so many outdoor cats in that climate she was a victim of the old morning-fan-belt-shredding, but, unlike most poor cats, she narrowly escaped with her life. Mom heard the shrieks when she started the car and feared the worst, but was relieved to see a survivor run from the scene. Cedar was certainly not much to look at after that. One ear was cut in two; the flapping top-half hung by a thin piece of skin for months. We didn't have the heart or guts to cut it off for her. Her tail was also broken and it dragged behind her in an undignified manner. We always knew her tracks in the snow by the heavily indented line snaking though her footprints. The tail eventually dropped off, like her ear, on another frozen night. She never got near the car again and was darn ugly from then on.

"Why don't you ever let your cats inside?" our city-slicker visitors would ask. People were moving into the area who questioned our generations of perfectly logical animal abuse.

"They're used to it," I'd say. "They just grow a lot of hair. If they can live through 54 below zero, like last year, they don't need to be inside." I didn't mention that the cats would try at every chance to get into the house, despite the likelihood of being caught. If they ever did get in they were tracked down by human bloodhounds and properly expelled from the premises. Summer or winter Mom would heave them by the scruff of the neck out the front door, sending them flying like a home-run hit. When Mom was ready to throw a cat we kids lined up for the performance. No matter what we were doing we'd drop everything when someone called out, "Mom's throwing Raisin!" or "Mom's throwing Cedar!" The winter performance was best, when the delinquent cat would, after a thirty-foot spinning flight, disappear completely into a sea of white. A short geyser of powder would shoot up, marking their landing spot, where ten seconds later a mildly ruffled cat would swim its way out of the depths, ready minutes later to try again to get back inside.

Only once did we miss the fact that a cat had entered the house. Cedar had stealthily managed to slip in the sliding door and hide somewhere until all signs of human life had gone. We returned home from softball practice that day to find Cheerios spread all over the kitchen. Mom threw a fit but could think of no punishment worse than a soaring toss out the door.

The ultimate pet event of my lifetime: when Max, our wimpy dog, actually barked.

On a brilliant crisp day in October, Kristen Bostrom, our neighbor from down the road, came over to show us her Halloween costume. Max was lounging in the front yard when Kristen walked up the gravel path from the road looking like a tower of Caucasian skin-tone fabric stuffed with fuzz. "What in the world are you?" I yelled to Kristen from the deck.

Before Kristen could answer, Max, whose voice we had never heard, jumped up and barked like she was rabid, with teeth bared and foaming at the mouth. The big peach-colored mound stood perfectly still in her tracks while Max continued her tirade. I did nothing. I was so stunned at Max's behavior I couldn't help but stare at her with my mouth open. Eventually poor Kristen had to fend for herself by lifting her costume over her head and saying, "It's me, Max. Hey, it's me."

Max did the doggie equivalent of turning beet red of embarrassment. She stopped barking as if she didn't know what had overcome her, looked sheepishly around to see who was watching, and slunk back over to her sleeping spot with her tail and ears tucked down. Not the least bit interested in the costume anymore, Kristen and I went over the whole scene together with amazement. We barely believed it. Max barked!

"By the way, what are you?" I asked after we'd sufficiently hashed over the incident several times.

"I'm a hand flipping the bird."

I am happy to say that all of our pets, without veterinarians or fancy food or even shelter, died of old age. Wimpy Max wandered off into the woods when she was in her teens, as did Priscilla who lived to be 16. Herman gave up his summer vacations when he got too old to hunt well, but one spring he left as if he was back in his younger days, setting out for life in the woods. He never returned.

After our horse, Casey, was too old to ride and a pain to take care of, we really did put him out to pasture. The Wymanses, who lived in the tiny nearby town of Milner, took him, saying he'd have a good home. Mom was convinced that they would immediately sell him to the glue factory, and that they'd only taken him from us to make us feel better believing he was going to a good home. We pretended he lived on and on at the Wymans', and never asked about him so we'd never know for sure.

Raisin, the friendliest, most human cat I've ever known, died of old age, too. After 12 years of being a tireless, faithful, protective mother of countless litters of kitties, and so loving that you couldn't help but be a better person when you were around her, she slipped away quietly into the sagebrush. Mom called me when I was away at college and told me she found Raisin in the bushes. Not since Wooch died did I cry over the loss of a pet. I bawled and bawled.

Cedar, the former beauty queen, became so old and ugly with so many conditions that she was basically a walking vegetable.

"Fred," Mom said one evening when Cedar was looking wretched and beyond help, "You've got to put Cedar out of her misery. Go look at her."

"She'll be alright," Dad said from behind his newspaper.

"Please go out and take a look her. She's not OK. Take a rock to her head."

After several more pleas from Mom, Dad reluctantly went outside. It was quiet for a little while. Suddenly out of the silence Mom heard three gun shots ring out from the woods.

"Thanks," she said when he came back inside.

Dad picked up his newspaper and went back to reading the sports section.

Little House Under the Snowbank

In 1961 Fred Duckels, my dad, saw beautiful Karen Staub, my mom, walking out of her dorm at Colorado Sate University in Fort Collins, and he asked the girl at the front desk to set up a blind date. On their first date they went to a restaurant and Mom was impressed by Dad's manners and his dry sense of humor, but mostly she was excited because he looked like Elvis Presley. In their first months of dating Mom had a good time making fun of his name and his country clothing with all the girls back at the dorm, but she liked him. She had always wanted a tall, dark, and handsome man who was the strong, silent type. Dad was all of these, but he could win a world championship for the silent part. Looking like Elvis didn't hurt either.

Mom was born in Denver and grew up on Albion Street, across from the City Park and the Denver Zoo. Her father, Henry Staub, was nearly 60 when she was born. He was a 6'4" dapper gentleman whom everyone described as "charming." He was an architect, and brought home a modest income. His elegant and graceful wife, Frances, was 30 years his junior. An eccentric and outspoken woman, she passed on her wild spirit and her incredible beauty to her daughter. Like her feisty mother, my mom was vocal and had a cursing habit. (Her language lost its shock value on us kids at an early age; we barely noticed it). From her mother's unconventional and progressive interests Mom gained an insatiable fascination for spiritual teachings of all kinds, Eastern philosophies in particular. But Mom was not interested in being fashionable or going to charm school like my grandmother. She preferred jeans and a sweatshirt to her mother's gowns and furs. She was athletic—a fantastic swimmer in her youth. She won medals and worked as a lifeguard for years. Mom has a younger brother, Bink, and they always seemed to me like best friends.

Mom went off to college to study physical education. There she become lifelong friends with her roommates and met my Dad. Mom thought Dad was a bumpkin. He drove an old, beat-up truck. She made fun of him for not being able to dial a telephone well; he was used to the old wooden wall-mount phone that required an operator. She admits that she may have found interest in him because he was different from her more refined parents.

When I asked Dad what happened when he and Mom first met he said, "We went on a blind date."

"What did you do?"

"Went somewhere and got beer."

"What did you like about Mom?"

"She was quiet."

"Mom? She was quiet then?"

"Yep."

"Is that it?"

"Yep."

"Wasn't she really pretty?"

"Yep."

Like I said, he is a quiet man.

After a couple of years of dating my parents "had to" get married, on account of me. They had a hasty wedding and moved to Dad's hometown, Steamboat Springs, where they set up house in Dream Island Trailer Park. Mom had been a big city girl, and had a hard time adjusting to small town isolation and living in a trailer. Due in part to Mom's badgering, they moved into a house after a year.

One-Four-Seven Spruce Street was a small, brick, two-story house with two big spruce trees in the front yard and a little fenced-in backyard. During the years we lived there I thought it was huge—our back yard went on forever, and climbing the stairs was a long trip. I see the house now, and it looks teenie. I don't remember a time when Mom didn't wish we could move. It seemed she was planning another new house not long after we moved into 147 Spruce. She complained that the kitchen was tiny (and it was; two people had to squeeze to get in) and after all four of her children had been born, we all six shared two very small bedrooms.

Mom's artistic talents showed up in everything she did, and she took pains to develop the tiny place into a fashionable home with orange paint on the walls, brightly colored curtains, and a kidney shaped coffee table surrounded by a curved turquoise couch set. She filled interestingly shaped bottles with colored liquids and arranged them in various vignettes. She collected art and weird trinkets from garage sales and placed them artfully around the home. I thought our house was groovy.

When we weren't in school we kids were required to be outside most of the time. The house was too small for four screaming kids to be running around; Mom liked to lie on the floor for hours and listen to Simon and Garfunkle and The Kingston Trio records, or read her stacks of books on metaphysics, Eastern and New Age philosophy, the occult, and popular self-help. By the time she was 27 she had four kids under the age of 7.

Summers for the kids meant long days in the back yard and running around the neighborhood. The sun didn't set until 9:30 at that latitude, and most days we had to be called in after dark. In those days kids could wander all over the neighborhood without anyone worrying. We played in the streets, wandered to other houses, rode our bikes as far as we wanted—without ever having to consult an adult. For entire summers we came in only for meals, to use the bathroom, or to sleep at night.

In winter we were in school, and in the evening Mom could be found in the kitchen preparing dinner and yelling at us to put our stuff away. We kids made sure to ask her a million questions, complain about being hungry, and get in her way as much as possible. Dad always worked late at his construction company and would come home smelling like diesel fuel and looking black all over. His hardhat left his sweaty hair squished into flat rings around head. Before he settled in for the evening, he'd go out to the coal shed in the backyard, get two buckets full of coal, and bring them down into the basement to shovel them in the furnace. He'd come upstairs and clean up only marginally, and when he removed his work boots we kids would run away with our noses pinched. Mom would yell at him to leave his goddamn stinky shoes outside.

Mom's dinners almost always consisted of either deer meat or elk meat. Dad and Grampa killed two of each during hunting season, and we were required to eat every last ounce of flesh from those creatures whether we liked it or not. And we did not. From kill to kitchen, neither of my parents knew how (or cared) to prepare our wild game in any sort of gourmet manner, so we choked down tough, gamy, and usually dry meat while trying not to gag.

Deer Burgers. Spaghetti with Elk Meatballs. Elk Casserole. Deer Steaks. Elk Jerky. Deer Stew. Deer Stroganoff. Elk Cacciatore. Elk Chili.

Mom tried to inject some variety to the limited assortment of protein sources, but even she admitted it tasted terrible. On the very rare occasions we were blessed with beef we considered it a fantastic delicacy and begged Mom to fix it more often. Both parents would retort with the usual financial statistics, and we'd shut up and enjoy cow while we had it.

Mom never failed to serve a square meal. The four food groups were always represented on our plate. Saying no for any reason was not an option, and cleaning the plate was also mandatory. I learned to like any and all foods, and still do.

It was not so easy for Debi. She hated lima beans. Her hatred of lima beans was legendary, and although I made myself love them, I loathed the times when Mom would serve them, because Debi would act as if we were pulling out her toenails one by one. She moaned and squirmed and stared at her plate. She cried and winced. She plugged her nose and tried swallowing them whole with milk to wash them down. She always managed to make them disappear from her plate, though, and I admired her tenacity.

After dinner, from the age of three on up, Debi and I were the dishwashers. At three years old (really) Mom trained us to wash the dishes—and wash them well. We had to kneel on a highchair to reach the sink in the early days, and I delighted in having such an important job. I looked at my reflection in the dark window and pretended I was in my own commercial for dishwashing liquid. I'd smile and hold up my detergent for the window to see. I'd hold up the plates when they were clean to show how well my detergent worked and happily place them in the drainer, satisfied with my superior product. As years passed my detergent modeling became more honed. I used more graceful—even sexy—hand movements to highlight my product and would hold the shiny clean plate close to my face while I smiled regally. I used phrases like, "softens your hands while you do the dishes" and "so clean I can see myself." Eventually the glamour faded—as anything would after doing it a thousand times—and by the time I was nine I dreaded dishwashing. I'd shuffle to the sink and complain and get it over with as quickly as possible. Sometimes I would try to conjure the old enthusiasm and do a commercial, but by then I could only have fun if I did an anti-commercial. "This detergent is so bad, it rots your fingernails and poisons your children. You'll never have to worry about eating again."

Dad would sit in his rocker after dinner, reading the paper and resting his famously smelly feet over the grate to the furnace. The furnace grate was our family hearth. For obvious reasons, the 3 by 5 foot grill was the hottest place in the house, and when the weather got really cold it was the only place in the house that was warm at all. Our little butts had grill marks on them most of the time. We kids would crowd onto the space, avoiding Dad's smelly feet, and try to stay on until the hot metal threatened to burn us. When we could no longer stand the heat (or the smell) we'd jump off into the arctic space surrounding the grate and cool down. Debi and I would have contests to see who could leave her hand on the grate the longest. I remember whole evenings spent pressing my hand onto the grate to see what kind of bright red geometric patterns I could make on my hands. Sometimes I'd just stare down to the basement and wonder what it was like down there, since we were never allowed to find out.

Sometimes we were able to look through the grate and see Mom's homemade wine factory. To save money on liquor, she'd fill glass gallon jugs with grape juice and leave them in the basement to ferment. An apparent part of the fermentation process involved the use of balloons, which she'd attach to the neck of the bottle. Then she'd wait for them to inflate. To involve us kids in the process, she used balloons that came in the shape of animals. We were told to tell her when the animals were full-size.

"Mom! The turkey's big!"

Mom would peer down into the basement.

"Yeah, thanks. It's not big enough yet. Let me know when it's really fat, like a Thanksgiving turkey."

"That bear's almost big enough."

"It sure is. You keep your eye on it."

We'd always ask if we could play with the balloons and she'd say we were playing with them, in a way. It was a game. They were too expensive to buy for kids. They'd just break. This way we got to enjoy them for a while.

We couldn't argue with that.

Only once did I see the grate pulled away from the furnace: when I dropped my Barbie shoe into black depths. I screamed when it fell; I'd just received a groovy outfit as a gift. The whole family knew about my insane obsession with

Barbie, and we all gathered to stare through the metal grid down at the delicate white shoe that lay on its side on the big dome that was the top of the furnace. I knew better than to make a scene or throw a fit. My parents just flat out wouldn't have it. I stared silently with tears welling up in my eyes. Without a word Dad left for a minute and came back with a screwdriver and oven mitts. He unscrewed the grate, and pulled it away from its hole with the mitts on. He lay on his stomach and reached down to try to pick up the little thing without burning his fingers on the furnace-top. Just as his thumb barely touched the plastic, it curled up into a little white melted ball. I could tell he felt bad, and it made me not care that I'd lost my precious new shoe. I felt so special that he'd gone through so much trouble for me. He left the little ball there and over the years it gathered dust and grime and turned dark grey.

Some summer evenings we would go for a ride. We kids didn't always like going for rides, but it was Dad's favorite pastime. I never thought it was strange that a couple evenings a week our family of six would pile into our station wagon and drive around Steamboat—just looking at things. Dad would hum his usual tunes constantly and in little snippets over the years we would learn them. "You load sixteen tons and what do you get? Another day older and deeper in debt. St. Peter don't you call me cause I can't go; I owe my soul to the company store."

Most of the rides we took were forgettable: driving down winding dirt roads through golden pastures in the cool evening; moving through the shade of towering willows along the raging Elk River; glorious sunsets seen though pristine pine forests; overlooking 50-mile vistas of fertile valleys from atop rocky peaks with rustling yellow aspen.

Most of the time we kids were fighting in the back seat or complaining about having to go to the bathroom. Dad always explained that we could travel the world over and never find a place more beautiful place than Steamboat. (He was probably right.) We'd seen those majestic mountains and meadows of gold since the day we were born. We grew numb to their grandeur; it all existed as just a backdrop for the more important matters that ran around our little heads: who could make the stupidest face or hold their breath the longest, what was on the school lunch menu next week, how to get a boy to notice you.

Our favorite destination was the graveyard, probably because Dad almost never went there. Perched on a hill just west of town, the graveyard was a small and humble place. No fancy entrance gate, no extravagant mausoleums or ostentatious stone carvings, no orderly rows of headstones; the place was more like Tombstone's Boot Hill than Arlington Cemetery. We loved to go there and see all the names of families we knew. There's a May! Compestine! I see a Zulevich! There's a pack of Zimmermans over there! Whether we were on a ride or not (even if it was nighttime and dumping snow), every time we drove past the graveyard we'd beg Dad to take us up there. He usually wouldn't.

Some rides were never to be forgotten. Three in particular stand out as historical events of soaring proportions. First, the infamous picnic my Mom bitched about our entire childhood. Thirty-five years later she still bitches about it. I am sure most women would join her.

Dad announced we were going on a family picnic, and Mom packed a basket with the usual stack of bologna sandwiches, fruit, and a generic brand of Oreos. Cans of generic pop were our drink. Keep in mind that Dad notoriously used rides as an excuse to go look at a construction job his company was working on. We spent many "rides" sitting in a parked car while Dad walked around an ugly dirt pile. For our special picnic Dad took us to eat at the site of his newly finished job—a sewer pond. We climbed a six-foot chain-link fence with barbed-wire to get to the site, sat on a dirt pile overlooking the waterfront view, and smelled the smelly smells one usually smells while sitting near a sewer pond. And ate food.

I saw nothing out-of-the-ordinary about our family outing. I was used to seeing Dad's job sites. Sewer jobs were not uncommon in the construction business. I had eaten many lunches out of a paper bag while tagging along on Dad's workdays. I couldn't understand why Mom was so upset. I might be wrong, but this picnic could possibly be the one thing that Mom complained about most in her years with Dad. From the day it happened for as long as I've known her, she referred to The Picnic at the Sewer Pond. I tried numerous times to get her to explain why it was so bad, but she'd look at me with eyes of horror—aghast that I'd even ask.

"IT'S A SEWER POND!" was her only explanation.

Occasionally, if we begged enough, Dad would take us to the city park on our ride. A string of parks connect along the Yampa River, and back then each had some mowed grass and a few swings. One park was the home of famous Sulphur Spring, a bubbling pool of stinky water that Indians used for medicinal purposes 100 years before. (There are numerous springs in the area, many named after a mineral as well. Steamboat Springs, just across the street from Sulphur Spring, was named by French trappers long ago for the tooting sound it made every so often.)

Now, before recounting this experience I must strenuously put forward that *we were young* when it took place. On this occasion, we'd driven out 20 Mile, a road that sings through peaceful farm country. We counted red-winged black birds, cattails, and cows. But mostly we pleaded with Dad to take us to the park, and this time he did. We pulled up next to the Stinky Spring and sprinted out to the swings. We played and shouted until the sun was nearly down, and Dad called us to get in the car. Debi and I ran over to him, but just before getting in we declared in unison that we had to go to the bathroom. At this time there we no facilities here.

"Oh just go behind the car," Dad said.

"We can't." I said. "Someone will see us."

"No they won't. Just go real quick."

We didn't bother to tell him that we both had to go number two, and he didn't ask.

"Well OK," Debi said.

We walked around the car while Dad turned his head, and we took kid-size steaming dumps side by side, dangerously near Sulpher Spring and right near the driver's door of our station wagon. Dad came around when we were finished and stood dumbfounded to see what we'd done.

"YOU POOPED IN THE PARK?" he roared.

"So?"

"You pooped in the park!?"

"You told us to," we said.

"You're not supposed to poop in the park!"

"You didn't tell us."

"I didn't know you were going to poop in the park!"

We looked at each other quizzically all the way home. I wondered what the big deal was. The incident must have seemed so insignificant to me, it slipped out of my conscious memory almost immediately.

The next morning Dad began his lifelong quest to tell everyone on Earth that Dori and Debi had pooped in the park. I wondered what in the world he was talking about. The accusation didn't embarrass me because I honestly didn't recall what he was talking about. He would bring it up to friends and family and laugh, and I would wonder where he came up with the story. I didn't argue; I just kept asking Debi why he kept telling everyone about it. She was young enough to have indecipherable answers to most everything, so I never got an explanation that satisfied me. I was the girl with the Dad who told everyone that I pooped in the park when I really didn't.

Years later when Dad's poop-in-the-park lie was all but a distant recollection, my subconscious finally released the captive memory. Debi brought it up when we were in our thirties—how Dad would never let go of it. Just as she mentioned it, I recalled the whole episode. It was a mammoth "Oh Yeah" moment. Suddenly the event became hysterically funny. I remembered our cute little poo piles by Dad's car door, and how perfectly normal we thought it was. I recalled all the times Dad told the story, and how I looked at him as if he'd lost his mind. To this day I think it would be fun to voluntarily forget things at will so I could relieve them years later through different eyes.

Before I recount the next tale, I must inject a statement about discipline.

Mom and Dad disciplined their children in much the same manner as most parents and teachers of their time and place. Punishment for wrongdoing was swift, decisive, probably cruel by today's standards, and very effective. After receiving consequences for a particular deed, a child would be considered exceedingly stupid for repeating the behavior. We knew grown-ups meant business.

Adults and children alike gauged punishments solely by their effectiveness, not their level of harshness. When my friends came to school solemnly relaying an account of what they got for being "bad," the reaction among the crowd was not "hey, your parents are mean" but "boy, I'll bet you'll never do that again." An adult's reaction to hearing another parent's punishment would be a nod of approval, an eyebrow in the air as a thumbs-up for creativity, and, like a judge flipping the card that showed a perfect 10, the statement "Well, now, Jimmy will never do that again, will he?"

Sammy Shots (not his real name) got caught smoking cigars behind the barn, and his dad made him smoke cigars until he puked. Pete Ploters (again, not his real name) the toughest boy in third grade, the one who wouldn't cry for anything, got caught chewing gum in class. He was made to walk from classroom to classroom with bubblegum stuck to his nose. He had to open the door to each room and stick his head inside while each teacher pointed to him and each room full of kids burst into laughter. When he came to my room I laughed too, until I saw he was crying so hard he was hyperventilating. Immediately the whole class stopped, dead silent, and watched him sob for a few seconds until the principal yanked him up by the shirt to move on the next room. Not one kid in Steamboat Springs Elementary School ever chewed gum again. I still won't get within 10 feet of a stick of gum.

Most parents had a belt (or strap, as my parents named their penalty weapon,) and at school we had a particularly merciless paddle for chastisement with which the principal gave "swats." The paddle was a wooden board with a handle, and an extra band of leather attached. While swatting, the leather hit the kid's fanny a split-second later than the wood, and was designed to inflict a little extra jolt of pain. The principal never got in trouble for swatting a kid. All parents applauded the procedure, and believed that if little Johnny had received swats, he must have deserved it. The only opinion we kids had about the matter is that we had better be good. We once heard rumor that the parents of a new family in town from California (whom we would label hippie ski bums, even though their income exceeded ours by a factor of 10) objected to their son getting swats. We whispered about what sissies they were.

One accomplishment of my childhood is that I managed to leave elementary school without ever receiving a swat.

On with the next story about rides.

On one of our more scenic dirt road drives, Dad finally got fed up with our noise-making in the back seat. Out one side of the car were rolling fields with hay bales casting purple shadows; out the other were rustling aspens, sagebrush, and high mountains in the distance. Instead of noticing that we could become millionaires taking calendar photos of everything we drove past, we were playing "monkey business" in the back seat. This was our name for the idiotic game we made up which involved doing ridiculous things with no purpose of any kind. Stupid noises, sounds, faces, poems, gestures, songs, jokes—anything absurd and silly. Monkey business could get loud. Dad had yelled several times from the front seat (which seemed 45 miles away to a kid in the very back of a monstrous station wagon) for us to "pipe down back there." His shouts had no effect on us. We were in the frenzy of monkey business fever—an unstoppable pastime. When it came to irrepressible laughter, no threats of an adult were worth slowing it down.

After a few more miles of "HEY! PIPE DOWN BACK THERE!" Dad stopped the car with a skid and said, "Get out."

"What?" we said.

"Now!"

We pleaded and cried that we would be quiet, but he wouldn't listen.

"OUT!"

Beginning to cry, we climbed out of the car and closed the door. We could hear Mom objecting in the front seat, but not very forcefully. Then Dad drove off.

"Run!" I screamed.

I remember a few times in my life that I ran like hell, and this was one of them. Debi and I were both wearing cowboy boots and pajamas, so running down a bumpy dirt road was difficult and painful. At first we could see nothing but the dust Dad had left behind when he peeled out. I coughed and cried and screamed and ran, ran, ran. I could hear Debi's screams behind me. I turned around to see her red, wet face some yards back. She was not only crying, screaming, and running, but also begging her big sister to wait for her. I was so scared all I could do was yell, "RUN!"

After Dad's dust cleared and the car disappeared around a distant bend I really panicked. I was sure night would come, and we wound die by the side of the road. Not for one second did I entertain the idea of slowing down or stopping. I ran hard. I barely noticed if I was out of breath or in pain from the cowboy boots. I just bawled and ran. Debi ran, too. I would look back at her from time to time and yell, "RUN!" but couldn't even consider slowing down for her. As she dropped further behind, her shrieks got louder and crazier. I just kept yelling at her to run. We kept it up for what seemed like a month.

Eventually Dad came back. As the car rounded a hill ahead Debi caught up to me. Our crying stopped immediately, and we stood together panting and drying our tears, kind of self-conscious about getting so worked up. Of course he'd come back.

"OK, it's OK, its over," I said.

When we opened the car door to get in, Mom and Dad had grins on their faces.

"You kids sure got far," Dad said. "You must've run two or three miles."

"I can't believe how far you ran," Mom said.

We said nothing.

"Are you going to listen when I tell you to be quiet?"

"Yes," we replied instantly and at the same time.

"What did you do back there?" Mom said.

"Ran," we both answered.

"Boy, you girls can run. You came a long way," Dad said.

"I just can't believe you could have run that far," Mom said. "Are you sure someone didn't pick you up and give you a ride?"

"Yep." I had no intention of emitting any sounds louder than a peep for a long time.

"Wow. I don't get it. I can't see how you could have gotten that far," Mom said.

"Dori and Debi are runners. They can run," Dad said.

Debi and I were only slightly proud of the running compliments. We were just glad to be back in the car. How swiftly we went from acting like crazed lunatics to sitting with small smiles in the back seat, soaking up attention.

Dad and Mom bragged for years about our running abilities. Debi and I kept our automobile monkey business to a whisper for the rest of our lives. Perhaps the incident influenced our later accomplishments of breaking high school track records.

I have two favorite memories from the old house. One is of my Dad carrying me to bed when I was eight. I had pretended to fall asleep on Mom and Dad's bed while watching TV. After the program was finished Dad came over to me, bent down and whispered, "Dori" in my ear. I didn't move. He wiggled me a little. I didn't move. I was eight years old and hadn't been carried to bed since I was tiny. I didn't for a moment think he would scoop me up; I thought for sure he'd speak my name louder or shake me a little harder. I was surprised when he gently slid his hands under me and lifted me into his arms. More than anything in the world I didn't want to let on that I was awake and ruin it. I looked really, really asleep. As he carried me, I treasured how warm he felt, and how fascinating it was to be floating in the air. I marveled at how strong he was. Mostly I cherished the fact that he didn't have to do it, but he did.

He carried me into my bedroom and tucked me in. I pretended to be sound asleep and never told him about it.

The other beloved memory is of Mom playing her ukulele. No one particular incident stands out. She played folk songs that she learned by ear from her records, or ones that she learned growing up. Simon and Garfunkle. Kingston Trio. The Brothers Four. Peter, Paul and Mary. The New Christy Minstrels. She had a beautiful voice, and I loved watching her fingers move over the strings. She had graceful hands. I would tell her so, and she wouldn't believe me. I would dream my hands would look like hers someday—lean, angular, and elegant.

She taught me a few chords, but my hands were too small to do well. I didn't want to learn because I preferred watching her play. I'd sit right in front of her while she sang and played, lost in the beauty of it. The harassed mother of four turned into a gypsy princess, a folk goddess, a star. Although in my eyes she became a transcendent being, she was unpretentious and modest. When complimented, she would insist she couldn't play well and could barely carry a tune, but whether this was true or not, I know it transformed her, if only for a little while.

Many of the songs she chose were sad, tormented, and inappropriate for children. This didn't occur to me at the time, but later in life I'd sing the old songs and realize what they were about. People (even children) died by freezing, drowning, and suicide. There were shipwrecks, hangings, knife fights, bounty hunts, murders of lovers in jealous rage, and loads of drinking songs. Filled with sexual innuendo, even the funny animal songs were naughty. I lamented through the songs of unrequited love, and chills ran through me when she sang mournful ghost stories in a minor key. She taught us to sniff as if we were snorting drugs for our part in "Cocaine Bill and Morphine Sue."

Although the words to many of her songs were dark, she ironically played them with an air of enjoyment. You could tell she found pleasure in imparting shocking tales with the sweet, tinny sound of her uke, as we called it. The miserable people she sang about were celebrated and honored in our little home, like relatives who'd never make it for dinner.

I still carry on the dark song tradition and teach them to my daughter.

Mom was dying for us to move into a new house; 147 Spruce was so small and drafty. She drew up several interesting, artfully designed plans for homes, but since Dad would be building the place, he poo-pooed all her ideas until the blueprints were simplified to a plain box with a sloped roof. They bought a four acre plot of land up Fish Creek Road—a gorgeous piece of property two miles out of town with no neighbors in sight—at the price of $200 an acre. Starting in my early childhood, Dad and Mom began constructing our new home at night after Dad got off work and on weekends. With Dad's equipment from his construction company, he dug the basement and poured the foundation, and he and Mom built the rest by hand. They didn't finish until I was a pre-teen. And the term "finished" is used loosely. We moved in when the four kids' bedrooms, which were all in the basement, had neither drywall nor carpet. We kids spent a few years with only studs to divide our rooms, and concrete floors to step onto when we got out of bed.

We were all overjoyed to move away from what was now to be called The Old House. I didn't spend one second grieving the loss of my childhood home. It was too small and too old. The New House may not have been completed when we moved in, but it was bigger and new.

While we were moving furniture from the Old House we found one last memory to carry with us. The bench behind the kitchen table was built into the corner: a plain, wooden, enclosed bench with slats, a few knotholes, and a hatch door that opened from the top. Debi had used it as her designated seat at the table ever since she graduated from the high chair. It had not been opened since we'd moved in ten years before. Because we could finally get to it with the table moved, Mom pried it open to see if we'd left anything in it. Inside we found years upon years of Debi's dried-up lima beans piled in a giant pyramid.

You're from Steamboat and You Don't Ski!?

In a town where Winter Olympians are bred like prize pumpkins, skiing was one of the first and most important things a child was supposed to master. I learned to ski when I was in kindergarten, on the playground at the Steamboat Springs Elementary School. We took lessons from our teachers on the very small hill adjacent to the school building.

I showed up for class with some seriously crappy ski equipment. I might as well have strapped two-by-fours to my feet with rubber bands. Actually, that's not far from what I had—faded light blue wooden skis with a u-shaped plastic strap in which my snowmobile boots would slip, and a metal spring-like coil that wrapped around the back of my boot. Mom had bought them at a garage sale. It's no wonder I didn't catch on to skiing. Mark Kinney and Heidi Ward had the newest equipment: leather string-up boots, and cable bindings, which actually held both the toe *and* the heel in place. By today's standards their gear would be considered utterly medieval, but compared to mine it was futuristic. They would swoosh to the bottom of the hill and into a sliding stop while I snowplowed one turn and fell. I would try to rotate one way, and my completely useless skis would fail to turn with me. I wasn't too keen on being out in the cold anyway, so I didn't fall in love with skiing the way so many of the other kids did.

The first alpine ski area in town was Howelson Hill, a one-run ski slope started in 1914 by Swedish ski enthusiast Carl Howelson. The ski area pours down the shady side of Emerald Mountain, just across the Yampa River from downtown Steamboat. One plowed strip through the trees and a rustic log hut at the bottom marked the only designated place to ski in Steamboat for many years. Some of Steamboat's favorite historical photographs depict Carl and his tanned skiing buddies in heavy wool Swiss-looking outfits, holding up their brown wood skis, with Howelson Hill in the background. The mountain looked pretty much the same when we skied it in the 1960s and 70s. My Dad skied Howelson in the 40s and 50s, as did his schoolmates Buddy and Skeeter Werner, and Moose Barrows, all famous Olympic skiers.

In 1963 a new ski area opened, on Storm Mountain, a few miles out Highway 40 towards Rabbit Ears Pass. Later named after Buddy Werner, who was killed by an avalanche in 1964, Mt. Werner was much bigger, better plowed, and higher tech than Howelson. It had a double chairlift and an A-frame cabin for a warming hut! It quickly became the preferred ski area for tourists, and most everyone else. Howelson was still open to the public, but was mostly used for training Olympic and World Cup skiers.

Although it is small, Howelson's resume is impressive. It is Colorado's oldest ski area. It has trained 47 Winter Olympians, 15 members of the Colorado Ski Hall of Fame, and six members of the National Ski Hall of Fame. Its training facilities have improved over the years and it now boasts the largest, most complete natural ski jumping complex in North America. And my Dad built those ski jumps!

In the 60s, as now, Mt. Werner was way more expensive than Howelson, and the Duckels parents decided the Duckels kids would stay in town to ski on the little hill. Debi and I spent many winter weekends at Howelson. It was a way to get out of the house for the day, and be completely out from under the jurisdiction of grown-ups for eight solid hours. Howelson, being on the shady side of the mountain and situated right next to the Yampa River, was even colder than the rest Steamboat, whose temperatures were inhuman anyway. Mom would drop us off in the morning and pick us up after dark, which was about 5:00. We'd usually be frozen solid.

Howelson was manned by one adult who sat in a log hut taking 50 cents a person for a full day of skiing. The duties of this person were to make sure people didn't lose limbs on the rickety lifts, and to drink hot chocolate. Twenty yards away from the hut was the lodge—a log building with concrete floors, a few picnic tables, a fireplace that I never saw lit, and palatial picture windows facing the mountain. Off to one side in the main room was a chalkboard with s-shaped figures drawn on it, used by the ski teams for instruction. This was where we thawed out every couple of hours. No food was offered, so we brought bologna sandwiches and an apple from home.

Rarely did we have to share the mountain with more than a handful of skiers. More often we had the hill to ourselves. Mt. Werner lured away all the people with more than 50 cents to spend on a day of fun, so Howelson became our own private place to raise hell and invent ways to make each other laugh.

There were two lifts at Howelson then. The Poma (pronounced PAH-muh)—a now-ancient contraption, consisted of long metal poles hung from a high heavy cable, each with a small round rubber "seat" at the bottom. To be towed up the mountain, you grabbed a pole, quickly thrust it between your legs, and then let the rubber seat pull your bottom up the hill while you stood upright on your skis. Due to the many dangers inherent in poma-riding this process is not recommended for young children. When we were little we used the other lift, which towed us up the baby run on the side of the mountain: the even lower-tech Rope Tow.

The Rope Tow was basically what its name implied. A rope on a pulley. We had to grab the rope, hold on, and go uphill. It sounded easy anyway.

The pulley was set at a particular speed and could only be slowed or stopped manually by the lone hut person, who sat nearly 50 yards away. Hence, the Rope Tow never stopped and it was never slow. As little kids we had to develop the gripping strength of a monkey and the balance of a tightrope walker to grab the rope while it was moving, withstand the little whiplash effect it had on our heads, and remain upright as we skied to the top of the bunny hill. We became quite adept at using the primitive apparatus, unless conditions rendered it more difficult, which was frequently.

Problems came when the rope would become icy, due to warm, mittened hands grabbing and melting the snow on the cord all day. No hands can hold onto ice. Debi would be halfway up the hill with me close behind when her tired little hands, worn down from hours of rope-clutching, would slip a few inches. Slipping under regular conditions always happens and is a natural part of the Rope Tow experience. But if the cord is icy where you slip, there is no grabbing back on. Debi, after a few seconds of desperately trying to catch the rope and sliding backwards would scream "I can't hold on!" and I would see her careening into me and scream "Get out of the way!" always too late. We'd end up in a heap on the tow path, with the heavy, cold, swift-moving rope running over our backsides, pulling the backs of our coats up and burning our skin. There were times when I'd pull the "Rope Tow Slip" on purpose, just to get a laugh out of Debi, but we both usually ended up getting hurt or too cold from lying in the snow battling an out-of-control, heavy, high-speed rope. If one of us pulled The Slip more than twice a day, whether by accident or prank, we'd be angry enough to sit out the rest of the day in the lodge.

There were days when the rope was so slick no one could grab it anywhere. Sometimes the rope would dig its own rut in the snow, so deep that you had to take your mittens off to pull it out and use it. More often than not, there was some challenge to contend with.

After kindergarten I had graduated from my blue wooden baby skis to a beat-up pair of gold wooden skis with paint peeling off the top. I got splinters from them a few times, but at least they had cable bindings which offered more control. As for skiing the bunny hill, I cared nothing about learning to turn, proper skiing form, or downhill etiquette. I started with my skis straight at the top, pushed off with my wooden and leather poles, and headed straight down the mountain. Other skiers be damned, I was an undisciplined rocket, and if anyone was in my way, we collided. My only skill was being able to stop at the bottom, so my days at Howelson—until we got older—were one quick up-and-down-the-hill run after another. I think Debi actually practiced getting better at skiing, but I was going too fast to notice.

Our few years of life on the Rope Tow were adequately amusing, but we knew there would come a day when we'd be able to graduate to the more adventurous Poma. Debi and I first spoke of it in hushed tones, wondering if we could handle it, talking about the ins and outs of getting on the thing. We told each other horror stories about accidents we'd heard of from other kids. But one day after Mom dropped us off and after she was far out of sight, we paid our 50 cents, donned our skis, and plodded over to the bottom of the big lift.

We looked up at the looming mountain.

We looked at the gangling apparatus waiting to be seized.

We argued about who would go first until I punched Debi and she agreed it would be her.

We looked around for a grown-up to supervise or give instructions or cheer us on.

The mountain was empty.

While she packed her way over to the Poma path, I shouted instructions about holding on and staying balanced—just like on the Rope Tow. Of course I knew nothing about Poma procedure. Debi allowed two poles to bonk her in the back before getting the nerve to try and grab one. Before she could put it between her legs, it had gone too far and it nearly yanked her hand off. She cried a little, mostly scared, and got up to try again. Like an army tromping over a fallen victim, several of the metal poles, one after another, smacked her head before she tried for another.

She snatched one in a panic, shoved it between her legs, and waited. The next second she was heaved forward with a jerk, and the suddenness of it made her lose her balance. It dragged her for a dozen feet or so, until she managed to set it free from her legs. It snapped back into line while she lay crying on the path with snow collected in her pants. We got her dusted off and set back to our task. If we didn't get this right, we'd be stuck at the Rope Tow for the rest of our lives.

We took turns at trying to get a hold of the thing, and after being bonked and dragged and whip-lashed or just falling over on our own, we finally learned how to get a hold of it. We didn't know, however, that unlike on the Rope Tow, you are not supposed to lean back or sit down until the spring inside it is taut. A few times of toppling backwards and being hit in the face by the next pole in line educated us swiftly in this matter.

Debi was the first one to start making her way up the slope in good form. Until this point, it hadn't occurred to us that we had to exit the Poma when we reached our destination. From below, I could hear her yelling something about how steep it was as she made her way up the slope, and I became a little worried when she began disappearing over the top of the mountain. I grasped a pole and hoped I'd be able to make it as well. Debi's victory must have stimulated my own sense of achievement because I, too, for the first time managed to hold on. I became more and more frightened as the trail got steeper and darker once in the trees. I could think of nothing worse than losing my balance and toppling backwards into the mean row of Poma poles. But by the time I began to round the top of the hill, I had gained confidence. It wasn't so hard if you kept your balance.

When the snow flattened out and it was time get off, I pulled the pole from between my legs and hastily threw it away from me, not wanting it to get caught on anything. The pole behind me whacked me in the head, teaching me to get out of the path once you exited. I found Debi waiting for me near the edge of the big hill, wiggling and blowing hot air into her mittens to keep warm. She'd figured out how to get off as easily as I had. But as I made my way over to her she said matter-of-factly, "We're in big trouble."

Since our foremost objective—a daunting one, we thought—had been to tackle the Poma, we hadn't anticipated any obstacles in our flight down the mountain. The main run at Howelson looked fairly tame from the bottom of the mountain, but we hadn't known that even the Olympic skiers that trained there considered it one of the most difficult runs around. To us, looking down from the top, it was Mount Everest. We could see all of Steamboat from up there. The huge warm-up lodge was tinier than an ant's fingernail.

After another solid punch in the arm, Debi decided to venture down the abyss first. I watched her try to turn, then fall, slide, get up and think, then fall, slide, get up and think several times before she resigned herself to slide down on her butt. Her practice at skiing skills on the bunny hill had at least given her the know-how to *try* to get down the slope in an upright position before giving up. I didn't have the guts to do anything but butt-slide from the beginning. I knew my only talent—flying in a straight line—would end in fatal disaster. Following Debi's lead, I butt-slid five yards at a time, to avoid gaining much speed. The wide-open run was icy, so when it came time to stop after letting myself go for five yards, I had to hurl my body against the slope and clutch the mountain like a cartoon cat trying to dig its claws into a steep tin roof.

We met at the bottom, cold and snow-covered, but triumphant. We could now ski the Poma!

For the next few hours, the lodge was headquarters to our strategic initiative to use the Poma but not have to ski down the face. We concocted a dangerous proposal involving an early exit from the Poma so we'd only have to tackle half the mountain and avoid the dreaded icy upper mountain. If we could get off before the Poma led into the trees, we could handle the less-steep lower mountain.

Warmed and mostly dry, we marched intrepidly back to the Poma, looking uphill at our proposed point of Poma departure. Exiting the Poma at the top had been easy enough, so we anticipated little difficulty in getting off at the halfway point. Thinking the undertaking would be undemanding after what we'd been through, I set out to catch a Poma pole first. Debi was right behind me. As the halfway point neared, I got ready to toss the Poma pole away from me and turn my skis. Suddenly it was time. I pulled the pole out from my legs and heard it snap back in position. But turning my skis to the left on a steep slope proved to be much more problematic than I had anticipated, and I hadn't factored in one essential detail: I had to immediately get out of the Poma path. I panicked. Screaming, with Debi headed uphill straight toward me, I hurriedly attempted to swing my skis around but instead fell over downhill. I tried to orchestrate my fall away from the Poma path, but my ski poles, which were wrapped around my wrist, caught on some part of Debi and pulled her down with me. We tumbled through the deep snow on the edge of the path with poles, skis, and little heads bounding down the hill in a great powder puff of white and cold. We came up laughing and after finding all of our gear, tromped back to the lodge.

It took us a few more weekends of Poma experimentation to learn the proper and perfect procedure for exiting early. It was a tricky process, one I'm not sure I would try today. But for years it was the only way we'd ski the mountain's face. Occasionally brave Debi would take her chances with the upper face, and she gradually became a better skier.

Most people who ski do so with intentions of improving their skills, enjoying the out of doors, cruising effortlessly or challenging themselves with difficult feats, or just looking good on the slopes. None of these objectives had anything to do with why we liked to ski. We just liked to goof off.

Not long after we discovered the joys of skiing The Face, Debi's friend and constant companion, Melanie Sprengle, introduced us to The Mile Run. We named the run this because we thought it was probably that long. (It is no more than a quarter mile, if that). The Mile Run began at the top of the hill and traced a narrow, winding, sometimes bumpy path around the backside of the mountain. No part of the path was terribly steep, so it became a source of endless fun for us goof-offs. We would make ski jumps to fly from; we'd gain speed for the "Bumpy Part", a Domino-like row of huge moguls (big snow bumps) that would knock us flat most of the time; we'd link our poles together and swing each other around the corners at high speeds; we'd race each other, try to lose each other, or just scream the whole way. Sometimes we'd stop and pretend to have a tea party, or make angels in the snow. No one but us ever took The Mile Run. It was totally ours.

Near the end of our favorite trail, off to the right, lay one of Steamboat's legends, Sulphur Cave. The entrance, perhaps fifteen feet across and high enough for a grown-up to walk into, was not up against a mountain, but lay against the earth. From Melanie Sprengle, who had three older siblings, we heard accounts of this mythic hole in the ground, and we grew to fear it absolutely. Our parents had warned us to never go into it, but would never give an adequate reason for the warnings. But Melanie had the ultimate Sulphur Cave story: *A boy rode his horse in there and never came out.* We shivered to think about it.

In the summer the place looked intimidating enough. It was a cave; it was dark; there were dripping stalactites visible from outside. But in the winter, due to the cold temperatures outside, it would pour forth steam—proof that there was something not good going on in there. We'd dare each other to get closer and even to go in, but even crazy Melanie would look inside only from afar. That place was scary.

Once in a while, Debi would act scared and say she heard a horse whinnying from the cave, or I would pretend I was careening out of control into the hole and stop just before it saying "Whew. That was close."

But mostly we left it alone. Some things are just too serious to goof around about.

The Mile Run necessitated that we always go to the top of the Poma lift. Riding it became second nature to us, and we felt quite imperial on the days when the Olympic teams would practice at Howelson and we'd be sandwiched on the lift between last year's medalist and this year's promising young upstart.

My little brother, Derick , came of Poma Age just before we quit skiing Howelson for good. (Peer pressure gave us the final push to graduate to skiing Mt. Werner.) For years we left Derick at the Rope Tow to fend for himself, but eventually we decided he was old enough to ski the Poma, probably because we wanted to torture him -- just a little. He screamed and cried and said he couldn't do it. To this day he will tell how terrified he was of The Poma. But we forced him to learn, and after having all the accidents and problems we had, he caught on and joined us up on The Mile Run. Most of the best winter memories, for all three of us, were on the backside of Howelson, just us, hollering "Hey, you gotta try this" or "Look out! Here I come!"

At the time, there were no tears shed when we made the move to start skiing Mt. Werner. We'd felt inferior for years, not just for skiing Howelson—that two-bit fleabag of a hill—but for having wooden skis and poles, wearing ripped and stained winter clothes, and doing something completely different from the other kids. Who cares that we were having more fun than anyone? Ski image is serious business in Steamboat Springs, Colorado. (Note: Today Mt. Werner is called "Steamboat" and the town is called "Old Town Steamboat." Some of this renaming business started years ago, and I still can't get used to it.)

In the 60's Mt. Werner was no more than a ski area. From town, at night, you could only see one light on the mountain. "There's the Ward's house," we would say when we looked up at the single twinkle on the shadowy wall of darkness. By day, if you drove out to the bottom of the mountain, you could see a few hotels such as the Inn at Thunderhead and the Ptarmigan Inn, as well as the couple of chairlifts that went to the top of the first mountain. Parking for skiing was available in a dirt lot adjacent to the lifts.

Today the mountain looks like the downtown of a major city at night.

I began skiing the big hill in junior high, and at first I stuck to the catwalks (gently sloped roads) and had fun, like at Howelson. But none of my skiing friends thought easy runs like Why Not and Right Away were cool enough. My siblings, the best skiing buddies in the world, were no longer available either. Debi now ran with a faster, more skilled bunch of skiers, and Derick was too young to be seen with. I didn't ski often, but when I did, Mercedes Thompson, an excellent skier, was my cohort. She'd wait patiently and ski intermediate runs with me instead of her usual experts.

Most importantly she'd chase after my ski when it got away from me. Sickening as it sounds, I had no safety strap to wrap around my leg (to prevent losing my ski when I crashed), and my old skis had no stops. I should never have been on a mountain with this most dangerous of ski hazards. Mercedes would have to fly at World Cup racing speeds to catch my runaway deadly spear when it popped off during one of my frequent falls. Once I wrecked on the very top of Heavenly Daze, possibly the longest run on the mountain. (When looking up at Mt. Werner from town, Heavenly Daze is the most visible strip on the front/center of the hill.) One of my skis took off like a missile and zoomed past little groups of skiers making their way down. If those innocent tourists didn't hear my terrified warning shrieks from the top of the hill before the ski whizzed by, they'd sure wake up when it passed them. They'd yelled things like "You're going to kill someone you idiots! Get off the damn mountain!" and "I'm going to report you to the ski patrol!" Mercedes would whoosh by them saying politely and sweetly, "Pardon me. Coming through." The ski stopped at the bottom of the run in a clump of bushes near the chairlift. (God help us if it had been directed seven feet to the left. Some oblivious tourist's first day of skiing would have left him or her headless.) Miraculously, no one got hurt, and I was never kicked off the mountain. But I was forced to ski Heavenly Daze with one ski that day. I butt-slid, something I was quite good at by now.

My best friend in seventh grade was Kelly Schell, another expert skier. She was too impatient to ever ski with me (not that I blame her) but she did sell me her old Spalding skis for fifteen dollars. I thought I had finally made the big time with my fancy, silver aluminum, twenty-pound short skis. Still light years behind the rest of the crowd in ski equipment fashion, it was a step up for me, and I couldn't wait to get out there and tear it up. My "new" Spaldings were scratched and dented, they didn't go fast, didn't turn well, and didn't look good, but they weren't wooden and they had a stop on them. On my first ride up the chairlift the tourist sitting with me laughed at them. I said, "What's so funny" and he said, "I'm not making fun. I just used to have a pair of those years ago." I glared at him.

The Spaldings served me faithfully for years, and except for a few laughs from other skiers and the fact that I could never go as fast as the rest of the crowd, I usually didn't care that they weren't so hot.

I lugged those heavyweight monsters to and from the ski area until one fateful night when I was a freshman in high school, after which I swore I would never use them again.

On a crisp, ultra-cold day in January, I skied all day at Mt. Werner, and didn't board the SST (Steamboat Springs Transit) bus back into town until after dark. Temperatures dropped another 10 degrees below zero. I got off the bus at City Market, which was then on Main Street, propped my skis and poles against the side of the store and reached into my pocket to get a dime so I could call Mom and have her come pick me up in town. (We lived then at the New House, up Fish Creek Road.)

I could not find my dime. I dug into every pocket and crease in all of my ski clothing but there was no dime. Tourists milled around the City Market parking lot, going in for groceries, waiting for the next bus, yelling about how drunk they were going to get at the Tugboat tonight. I looked around for a familiar face; perhaps someone I knew would give me a ride or loan me a dime.

I paced back and forth, looking worried and upset, hoping someone would ask me if I needed help. No one noticed me.

A tourist came over and started asking about my antique skis, but I didn't have the guts to ask for money. As he spoke amiably and I answered his questions—yes, I really was born here, yes, there really is a school here, yes, it is often this cold—I yearned for him to ask how I was getting home or why I was standing around at the supermarket. But he didn't.

Finally, after an hour of agonizing worry and colder and colder temperatures, I got the guts to approach a tourist. He turned around and smiled at me and I just stood there. I couldn't do it.

I walked glumly over to my skis and poles, hoisted them over my skinny shoulders and headed toward Fish Creek Road. Clumping awkwardly down the street in my ski boots, my burdensome, heavy skis were already digging into my shoulder bones before I even got to the bottom of the hill. My hands and feet felt like popsicles. I was exhausted from skiing. I was starving. And I felt like a loser for not asking someone for a lousy dime. Our house was two miles up the mountain, there were no houses to give light along the way, and there was no moon. It was then that I realized I had to go to the bathroom.

I waited a few minutes at the bottom of the hill thinking someone might give me a ride. No one came. I knew that once I was part way up the hill no one could stop on the icy road and get going again. I set out, wishing someone would just shoot me as they drove by. No one did. Going was extra slow wearing my bulky, stiff boots and carrying my despicable skis and poles. I'd stop every 20 yards and drop my load to bang my mittens together and stomp my boots to try and get some feeling into my extremities. I'd then scrape the built-up snow off my boots with my pole, switch the Spaldings to the opposite shoulder and re-commence with my suffering. I thought of Jesus carrying that cross and felt sorry for him. A couple times I had to drop everything to cross my legs and stop myself from peeing my pants. For an hour and a half I was tortured by the crunching sound of my boots on the snow and my own heavy, white breath. The snowy hills and fields sparkled beside me and the Milky Way was brilliant and I hated all of it.

By the time I got to Huckleberry Lane, the last quarter mile, I would hurl my equipment on the ground and kick it before switching shoulders. I started to cry a few times, but made it stop straight away so I didn't waste energy.

Four hours after I left Mt. Werner, I threw my ski equipment down on the driveway and walked in the front door of our house. Mom and Dad, usually oblivious to the whereabouts of their kids, came running over to me and asked what had happened. Dinner had been eaten, and all the kids were getting ready for bed. Without answering, I stumbled toward the bathroom fumbling to tear off my mittens and hat and scarf with my completely numb hands. After peeing, which felt like heaven, I staggered over to the heat register in the living room. Layers of clothing were tossed in a pile before I sat in my long underwear and started thawing out. I told Mom and Dad the whole story, and they genuinely felt bad for me. Neither of them questioned my inability to ask for a dime. I don't think they would have done it either.

As soon as I'd defrosted and eaten a hot dinner—long after all the other kids were in bed—I picked up my wet clothes to put them in the dryer. I found a dime in a little pocket in my jeans.

I refused to ski again until I got another pair of skis. It was hard enough for my parents to buy new jackets for four kids every year, so I never did get another pair. I would rent them on the rare occasions that I cared to brave the ski slopes. By high school I decided that playing basketball was better than freezing my butt off, so I became almost a non-skier.

Poor Derick inherited the Spaldings. He still talks about how heavy they were and how, when he'd be chasing his friends down a catwalk like Flat Out, the rutted, wasted old things would just come to a stop.

Fed up with freezing half to death and rotten ski equipment, I never bought a season pass to Mt. Werner, and sometimes I only skied once or twice a year. Out-of-towners nearly started crying to hear that a native didn't ski. When I went off to college I must have heard on a daily basis the question that haunted me for years and that no amount of explaining would satisfy, "You're from Steamboat and you don't ski!?"

Holy Name

Every Sunday morning at eight o'clock Dad towed us kids to the Holy Name Catholic Church for mass. We would have rather slept in most of the time, but we never argued because we knew it was useless. Before Derick and Dana were old enough to go, Mom would dress Debi and me in matching Sunday-goin'-to-meetin' outfits complete with white hats with a ribbon hanging off the back and little white gloves. Not a Catholic, Mom would send us off and stay home to make pancakes while we were gone. The ladies at church fawned over our cuteness. As we grew older Mom's enthusiasm for having cute kids waned. Eventually we just threw on whatever wrinkled, stained jeans and t-shirts were lying on the floor from Saturday. We fit in much better with the other churchgoers.

Dad would hum one of his top ten favorite songs on the way to church in his pick-up (usually Jingle Bells or White Christmas, even in July) while we stared sleepily out the window. If we got a parking space up near the Church he'd say, "Hey! We got the governor's spot today!" If our space was not near the church, he'd say, "Hey! The governor must be here today. He's in our spot."

Holy Name, the only Catholic church in town, is a small brick building, with a steep tin roof. No church in Steamboat was fancy back then; all religions worshiped in small brick buildings, except for Euzoa Bible Church. It was made of wood and had a steeple. But, not long after one of the Euzoa Bible accountants got caught embezzling money, it was hit by lightening and changed thereafter to a bed and breakfast.

After dunking our hands in holy water (and flicking it on each other) we'd follow Dad like little ducklings to the sixth row, left hand side of the church. Always the same pew unless someone else was there, in which case we sat in front of them. The church was then never crowded except for Easter and Christmas, so we had our pick of the place. I'd pretend to pray for a few minutes like all the other adults, except I was too chicken to interlock my fingers the way everyone else did. The nuns at catechism had taught us to hold our hands with our fingers pointing straight up, thumbs folded over each other, like Mary and Jesus did in the pictures. I'd been told I'd go to hell for so many other things, I was certain I'd wind up there if I held my hands the wrong way while praying. I rationalized that the grown-ups must have gone through some sacrament that allowed the interlocking finger technique. Maybe marriage or something.

My main reason for listening to the priest during church was to see if I could memorize the whole mass. My little lips would move along with his words and I'd recite the audience responses with vigor. By third grade I had it wired except for the Apostle's Creed. I kept mixing up the "God from God, true God from true God" part. I thought that whoever wrote it must have been playing a tongue twister trick on us all.

I also liked to privately rate the alter boy's performance and showmanship. Did he properly fold the tablecloth or did he leave edges hanging out? Did he fidget on the bench or act pious with his hands in the proper straight up position? And most important: Did he ring the bell exactly when the priest raised the chalice and let it dangle until it was quiet? I obsessed over the bell-ringing job. An alter boy who missed his cue or clanged the bells loudly or slammed them down in the carpet lost gobs of points on my alter boy rating system. I think Tom Southall won the lifetime alter boy achievement award but he never knew it. He gained lots of extra points because he was good-looking.

Another pastime I liked was counting the ribs on the emaciated Jesus that hung on the cross above the altar. This kept me busy until I learned in school how many ribs people have.

The first priest I remember was Father Funk. He scared me to death. He was the world's only fire and brimstone Catholic priest. He'd lean over the pulpit and yell and his eyes would bug out of his head. I don't remember one word he said; I was too busy being frightened. After church when all the parishioners would meet in the church basement for donuts and coffee, I'd stay as far away from Father Funk as possible, even though his red-faced ranting had changed into smiles and handshakes.

"Why is he so mean?" I asked Dad.

"He's not mean. He's just gets excited," Dad answered.

Only once did Mom join us for mass. Perhaps it was Christmas or Easter, because the church was packed, forcing us from our sixth row seat to the very front row. Our whole family sat lined up only a few feet from Father Funk's pulpit. One of Mom's babies began crying softly, stimulating Father Funk to stop yelling, point directly at my mortified mother and motion for her to exit the chapel. Dad commenced to lead the way out of the pew but Mom wouldn't budge. Red-faced, she looked Funk straight in the eye and shook her head no. She refused to walk dejectedly away in front of the whole congregation with her kids trailing behind her. We remained in our seats for the entire mass, and of course Mom never came back, and of course Dad never asked her to.

The priest who took charge after Father Funk left was gentle and nice. Instead of being petrified during the homily, I was painfully, excruciatingly bored. I kind of missed old Funk.

Mass memorization and alter-boy rating were the least entertaining of my church activities. Most of my time my siblings and I strove to cause as much trouble in our pew as possible without my Dad noticing. Dad seemed to drift away into Catholic Land at church and was barely aware of our existence, let alone our naughtiness. We loved Dad at church. He never scolded more than a whispered "Hey." We could have set the bibles on fire and he would have whispered "Hey."

"I dare you to touch that guy's coat," I'd whisper to Debi.

She'd touch it.

"Now some skin. Touch his hand."

Giggles from both of us. The churchies around us looked our way.

"I can't reach it," Debi said after trying.

"Touch it when he stands up.'

At the next ALL RISE part Debi reached up and poked his hand with her finger. He turned around and grinned at her as if it were an accident. Debi turned beet red. Uncontrollable whisper-giggling from both of us.

"Hey," said Dad.

This scenario and variations thereof occurred seven or eight times a mass. Our goal was to come up with new and original ways to make each other laugh, week after week, year after year, true God from true God.

We'd lick each other's tongues.

We'd see how far down the pew we could scoot before Dad would whisper "Hey." (Usually we could sit 15 feet away for 15 minutes without his noticing.)

We'd see who could sing hymns the loudest. By the end of the song we'd be shouting.

We'd see if anyone noticed if we put back on our hats, coats, mittens, and scarves in the middle of mass. They noticed. Dad said "Hey."

We'd take our snowmobile boots off and stick them under the legs of the kneelers so that when the ALL KNEEL part came, the whole row would have to figure out why the kneeler wouldn't go down.

After we were old enough to take communion, we'd dare each other to lick the priest's finger when he placed the communion wafer on our tongues.

We'd have a contest to see who could keep their wafer from disintegrating the longest.

We'd start clapping when the priest finished his homily. The whole congregation would follow suit until they quickly realized that Catholics don't clap. The applause would trail off and people would shrink a little with embarrassment.

A more strategic ploy that took timing and cunning was to try to get the whole parish to stand up at the wrong time. We'd wait for the part of mass with a good mix-up of ALL RISE, ALL KNEEL, and ALL SIT. We'd pick a good break in the words, which might be confused with a good time to RISE. Then we'd stand up together as if it were perfectly proper, and watch everyone follow our lead. Seconds later the crowd would laugh, not knowing who had started the whole mess-up, and sit back down again. There would always be some super-perfect dutiful holy roller woman who wasn't fooled. She'd stay seated and have a look on her face like she felt sorry for all of the rest of us heathens. I think we were too overwhelmed at our powers of persuasion to giggle much after the Stand Up Routine. We'd save the laughter it until we got home.

We'd cause the most trouble when Dad left the pew. He was a Knight of Columbus and sometimes had to read a passage from the Bible or take around the collection basket. We took this opportunity to have sliding races up and down the pew, tuck bibles and booklets under the seats, fart and burp loudly, and pinch each other. One of us would say, "Straighten up!" and we'd jerk into a stiff-as-a-board position, then laugh our heads off. Other parishioners took it upon themselves to discipline us by leaning over and shaking their heads at us. It never worked.

One Sunday, when the time came during mass to shake the hand of those around you and say, "Peace be with you," Debi and I came up with an ingenious plan to humiliate little Derick who was perhaps three or four at the time. "Poop be with you" Debi said to him when she shook his hand. "Poop be with you," I said when it was my turn. "POOOOP?" he yelled at the top his lungs. Debi and I fell into a laughing fit in the pew. The whole church uncharacteristically chuckled, too. Dad said "Hey."

Derick took the brunt of all kinds of harassment, most of which I have blocked from my memory, probably out of guilt. Mostly we'd pinch him until he squealed, to which Dad retorted with a pinch for Derick.

For a reason that Dad never explained we eventually relinquished our regular seats in the sixth left pew and started sitting up in the balcony. No one sat in the balcony except for people who didn't want to be seen. Dad cared even less how unholy we acted once we changed seating arrangements. He still whispered "Hey" or pinched us, but our conduct had to escalate to extra-wicked to warrant it. The only other churchies to scold us now were the ones 25 feet below us in the main chapel, and far away as they were, we were sometimes bad enough to merit unpleasant looks from them. The worst of all our dirty deeds was when one of us (I wish I remembered who) spit his or her chewed gum onto the head of a bald man below us.

When Dana became old enough to start coming to church, Debi's and my hazing techniques had mellowed. I had a mothering attitude toward Dana and refused to hassle her. The little kids formed a team whereby Derick took out on Dana all the persecution that had been inflicted upon him. They sat next to each other, near Dad, and continued the legacy of pinching and being pinched. We big girls were old enough by then to become lost in our own thoughts of school or boys or daydreaming.

Extracurricular activities at Church included the following: Coffee and donuts after mass, church potlucks, Knights of Columbus Pancake Breakfasts, and catechism for the kids every Thursday after school.

Catechism was supposed to be the place where I learned from the nuns about the meanings of the rituals and customs and beliefs of the church, but perhaps like most children, I jumbled the information into an unsound mess of ridiculous notions. First, I latched onto Sister Mary Ann's statement that in heaven one could have anything one's heart desired. This was the most enticing bit of information I acquired in all my religious instruction and it led to the development of an elaborate fantasy world involving Barbie. The only heaven I could imagine was one in which I was the owner of every kind of Barbie, all of her accessories and outfits, her cars, her homes, Ken and Skipper, and especially her official carrying case that doubled as a pink armoire with little hangers for her clothes.

I was more than happy to recite the seven sacraments; I loved to memorize everything. Baptism, Communion, Confession, Confirmation, Marriage, Holy Orders, Extreme Unction. Extreme Unction, or The Anointing of the Sick, or Last Rites, was my favorite because it had a nice sound to it. But I was a little disappointed that I would not be able to experience all of the sacraments. Why did we have to learn about Holy Orders if it was only for priests anyway? I reasoned that it was left in there to entice boys to become priests someday. For a short time I thought I would surely become a priest if I was a boy, so I could say I completed all of the sacraments.

I learned to dread the few times a year when the priest would come to catechism and announce that we were going to go through the stations of the cross. If only we didn't have to stand up through the entire process! Father So and So would lead us around the perimeter of the pews in the church dressed in his robes and carrying a big stick topped with an ornate gold cross. We'd stop at the little stations—

each a small, wood framed print of Jesus going through the motions of being crucified—while the priest or one of the nuns read from a little book about what was taking place in the picture. It was the same story each time we went through it, and it would have been bearable had we not had to stand the whole time. I'd look out the windows or stare longingly at the pews where I'd like to sit down and daydream about Barbie. The only part of the ceremony I looked forward to was the part about the actual gory crucifixion. "Have you ever pricked your finger with a pin? Remember how painful it was? Well just think of how it must have hurt Jesus to have big stakes driven clear through his hands!" These were my favorite words of the narrative and the only ones I remember today.

"What's the difference between Holy Water and regular water?" one bold catechism student asked one day.

"Holy Water has been blessed by a priest," Sister Mary Ann answered.

"Does it taste like regular water?"

"We don't drink Holy Water. We use it to cleanse our spirit when entering God's church."

"So what's different about it?"

"It's been blessed. Next question."

After that one person had dared to ask about holy water, I became curious about it, too. Did it taste like perfume? Could it cure a headache? Would you get sick if you drank it? What would happen to you if you poured it on the ground? What did the alter boys think about Holy Water? Was I going to hell for flicking it on my sister?

"Bless me Father for I have sinned. My last confession was two weeks ago."

"Go ahead."

"I flicked Holy Water on my sister."

"Say three Our Fathers and three Hail Marys."

I did.

I guess I won't be going to hell. Over that anyway.

Holy Water was a mysterious, hallowed, sacred thing. But nothing compared to the Tabernacle. In our church, the Tabernacle was a small compartment like a safe, encased in an elaborate, flamboyant, massive wood altar. It was housed in the space we called "The Cry Room." With a glass partition between it and the main chapel, The Cry Room was designated for mothers with loud babies. Most of our catechism classes were held in there, and we gazed at The Tabernacle with wonderment while the nuns spoke of it with reverence.

The Tabernacle is the most sacred place in the church.

The body and blood of Jesus are inside the Tabernacle.

Only a priest can open the Tabernacle. No nuns.

Always make the sign of the cross *and* genuflect when you cross in front of the Tabernacle.

The Tabernacle scared the crap out of me. What did they mean, the body and blood of Christ? How'd they get their hands on that? Why no nuns? It must be really scary if a nun can't get near it. Once in a while I would forget to genuflect before entering a pew, or forget to make the sign of the cross after communion, but I *never* forgot to do *both* when in front of the Tabernacle.

The Knights of Columbus Pancake Breakfast, which was held a few times a year, is not really worth mentioning except for the fact that I got to see the principal of my elementary school in an apron. Mr. Fitch was feared by most kids at school as the man that gave "swats," or hard spankings with a paddle. Seeing him in girl clothes serving women and children breakfast was a treat I savored, only because I could go to school and announce that I'd seen it. My Dad also cooked and served pancakes in an apron, the only time in my life I've seen Dad working in a kitchen.

Potlucks were held more often than the K.C. breakfasts, and I always looked forward to them with enthusiasm. I considered the mushroom-soup casseroles, mayonnaise-noodle salads, and Jello-fruit-cocktail molds to be haute cuisine delicacies, and thought church potlucks were the height of culinary enjoyment. I remembered which recipe was made by which old lady (anyone over 30 was old), and would be sorely disappointed if one of them couldn't make it to the festivities.

After we'd stuffed ourselves like ticks with starchy food, we kids would run upstairs to play outside. More often than not there was snow on the ground, prompting the usual snowball fights. With barely any winter clothes on to speak of, we'd pummel each other ruthlessly, until we were frozen, soaked, exhausted, and happy. One time Joe Green threw a snowball at Jody Arroyo while she was screaming at full volume and it landed in her mouth. She stood stunned, eyes wide, for a moment with an oversized white blob for a mouth. I wanted to feel sorry for her but I fell on the ground laughing until I couldn't breath while she picked it little by little out of her jaws. I told Father about my sin in confession a few weeks later. I got quite a few Hail Marys for that one.

By the time I reached high school age, my respect for the sacrosanct had diminished considerably. My sisters and I conducted skits at home for our mother that involved blasphemous re-enactments of the sacrament of communion. Debi would dress in sheets to play the part of the priest while Dana and I walked piously up with our hands in upright prayer position for our share of the body and blood of Christ. Debi would raise a banana slice in the air and say, "The body of Christ," wait for Dana to close her eyes and open her mouth, and then brutally smash and rub the banana all over her face. No matter how many times we repeated the skit Mom never failed to laugh her head off.

There were two girlfriends in my school grade who were practicing Catholics: Cathy Miller and Katie Lee. Cathy, the smartest, nicest, most well-behaved girl in school wouldn't take part in any sacrilegious deeds, but Katie was as interested in devaluing Catholic dogma as I was. We made up obscene names for the nuns, would sneak away from youth group to partake in mind-altering substances (which turned the normally boring meeting into a barrel of laughs), and ate communion wafers for afternoon snacks. We truly found out that God herself would not strike us dead for our sins the day we snuck into the priest's vestibule with a non-Catholic friend, Jill Wood. Jill had no preconceived ideas about the sanctity of church props and proceeded to try on the priest's robes—even the purple ones, used only for Lent—and model them for us. Katie and I laughed timidly, wanting to burst open with glee but horrified at the sight before our eyes. A non-Catholic *woman* in the priest's clothes! Jill's performance spurred us on to take at least a small risk. We drank a full cruet of holy water.

"What does it taste like?" Jill asked.

"Warm tap water," Katie and I replied.

"So what's holy about it?"

"It's blessed," I said, as if she should know.

"What did you think it would taste like?" Jill said.

"Perfume," I answered.

"Soda," Katie said.

"So now you know. It's just water. Let's get out of here."

We replaced the cruet with tap water, joking about how people would have terrible days after touching it because they thought it was holy when it really wasn't. As we walked into the cry room, Jill thought she'd have a little more fun by opening The Tabernacle. Katie and I froze with horror. *Not the Tabernacle*! Luckily it was locked and we left the church laughing about how stupid it was to believe in holy water.

Pop, Candy, and Bulldozers

When we were little, Duckels Construction was, too. A few miles west of town, out Elk River Road, was the home of my Granny and Grampa, and along side their home was the construction yard of the company they ran with their son, Fred—my dad. It was one of the dominant playgrounds of my youth. Dad and Grampa employed hired hands, but labored harder than any of them, running equipment, fixing equipment, and doing anything big or small that needed to be done. I don't remember Dad and Grampa ever working an 8-hour day or a five-day workweek; it was always considerably longer. Granny never rested either. She was in charge of the books, the housework and yard-care, feeding everyone, and babysitting her grandchildren who came to call a few times a week.

As kids we paid scant attention to the toiling adults around us when we visited. "Granny's House" was like Disneyland to us. From our first step in the front door, we were enthralled with our surroundings that, in retrospect, seemed enticing mostly because they were different from home. Plastic runners covered the carpet in the front room, and transparent sheeting draped the furniture. With blackened construction workers entering the house at all hours, Granny had devised this method for cleanliness, an appointment I considered to be the pinnacle of futuristic luxury.

Without bothering to greet our grandmother when we'd arrive, we'd holler, "Can we have pop and candy?" Granny would always say sure, and we'd sprint back to the three horizontal deep-freezers lined up in a room behind the kitchen, a room we called "the room with the candy." Filled to the top of the enormous appliances was every kind of candy bar and treat we'd ever heard of, and we were allowed to eat as much as we wanted. These freezers were an overblown result of Granny's penny-pinching obsession. She took the term stocking-up very seriously. A "candy on sale" sign meant to Granny, "take home all the candy we have." Running out of candy for the grandkids was not going to happen.

We never had the patience to wait for our frozen candy to unthaw, so we gnawed on chocolate hard enough to chisel away a tooth, and popsicles so cold they'd freeze to our lips. Pop was stacked in the basement by the case—the wooden ones with glass bottles—and we believed that Granny stocked it only for us kids. I drank six or seven bottles a day, added to various combinations of candy bars, hard candies, ice cream treats, and popsicles. We spent our days at Granny's house stuffed, sick, and on a roller coaster of sugar highs and lows. Of course, we considered Granny to be the nicest lady in the world.

Grampa would sit in his easy-chair after work and joke with us, and sometimes tell us the story of how Duckels Construction came to be.

In 1944, not long after my aunt Mary Ann was born and my dad was six years old, Tom and Mary Duckels moved their family from Denver to Steamboat—a place Tom had only seen once, as a child, and fallen in love with. It was beautiful and peaceful, and his brother Jack sold Tom a few foxes to start his own farm up in Steamboat. This was Tom's dream come true then. They moved to the mountains in an old Chevy beet truck.

Until they found land to buy, they stayed in the Spring Creek Motel on Main Street (where the post office later stood for years and now the Pilot Office Supply.) Finding a piece of land was difficult; they could find no one who wanted to sell, but finally a man named Carver sold them a parcel of property on Elk River Road for $100 an acre, an outrageous sum at the time. People in town talked about the high-cost purchase for years. On the property was an old one-room cabin, built in 1903, with saggy floors and a door one had to hunch over to get through. They lived in the little shack until they built a new home in the early 1950s.

The fox farm thrived for a few years. Silver fox was in demand at the time, and expensive. To feed their foxes, they bought old horses from farmers for five or six dollars apiece and slaughtered them.

The fox farm came to an end when fox fur suddenly became unpopular overnight, and people turned their favor toward mink. There was no money to be made in their business, and they were forced to let all of their foxes go. Granny stayed inside the cabin while Grampa let them lose. She couldn't bear to see them run away into the sagebrush. Grampa told us that silver fox seen today in the Yampa

Valley are descended from their farm foxes, and new unusual breeds are being seen after half of a century of mixing with the native fox. Back in Denver, Grampa's brother Jack had the foresight to start raising mink before the fashion change and ended up having a huge farm of 25,000 mink. For years he was the sole provider of mink for Neiman Marcus.

Although he despised working for someone else, Grampa went to work in the Mt. Harris Coal Mine west of Steamboat. He and Granny bought an old restaurant, the Mountain Home Café, located on Main Street, for one hundred dollars. They tore it down and used the lumber to build a house on their property. By themselves and only in their spare time, they hand-mixed and hand-poured cement for the foundation, and removed the old nails from the restaurant lumber and straightened them to use again. Grampa hauled beautiful red stones from the quarry out by Hahn's Peak for the exterior; he was given a portion of the load in exchange for hauling the stone into town for the quarry company. The house, built for next to nothing but hard work, was one of the most beautiful houses in town at the time.

Determined to have his own business, Grampa, with Granny's help, began his own company on the side. Work was scarce, and the demand for new construction low, but he and Granny began their own construction company with a 60-dollar hand mixer and a shovel. They set up shop about 100 yards away from the new house. Grampa had to travel all over Colorado on weekends and after his mining job to find work. He made 60 dollars profit in his first year.

Gradually, as Steamboat's population swelled with the skiing industry, construction became one of the most active businesses in town. Over the years Granny and Grandpa's company, *Steamboat Ready Mix*, grew in size and profits, but expanded even more after Dad graduated from Colorado State University in Fort Collins with an engineering degree. He came home with new ideas and changed the company name to *Duckels Construction*, specializing in dirt work and heavy construction.

After Grampa told his stories, he'd usually doze off while sitting up and snore so loud we'd have to move into the kitchen to hear ourselves have a conversation.

We kids grew up in and around construction equipment. When we were babies, Dad held us in his arms as he pushed dirt with the loader, and taught us to work the machinery when we barely knew how to walk. He'd scoop three of us at a time in the backhoe bucket so Mom could take our picture, waving from our roost high in the air. We knew all of the names of various types of equipment and what they did before we knew our alphabet.

Retired equipment was never hauled from the yard; it was merely permanently parked in one area to gather dust, rust, and weeds. The yard was not pretty. Rutted dirt roads stained black with diesel fuel led through fields of daisies. Mingling in the flowers were old cars and trucks, concrete mixers, backhoes, bulldozers, scrapers, loaders, scrap metal and discarded parts. When I was in elementary school, the yard earned the title, "Eyesore of the Week" in a caption in the *Steamboat Pilot*, under a photo of what looked like an overgrown junkyard. Dad and Grampa quickly removed much of the old equipment and tried to keep the yard cleaner, but it was never nice to look at.

In the center of the yard was a pond surrounded by willows, at first glance an oasis in the middle of an industrial graveyard, but closer inspection revealed the surface of the water to be a fluorescent rainbow-colored oil slick mingling with stagnant, smelly, green slime. We kids were always told never to drink from or play in the pond, but occasionally we'd stir it with a stick, hoping to find, underneath the layer of toxic waste, crystal waters pure enough to drink or jump in. But no. Below the contaminated surface was only more blackish green water.

The pond was a central figure in our Granny's House experience. When I was in fifth grade and should have been old enough to know better, I decided to try a sip. No one else was around, I was thirsty, I didn't want to walk over to the house, what could one little sip do? I scooped up as much as my cupped hands could hold and ducked behind the willow tree to test it. As I tipped my fingers up to my mouth, I breathed in a swampy, diesel odor. I sipped and swallowed, then wiped my hands on my jean shorts. One second later I emitted a loud cough into my hands and found four small black bugs that I had choked up. How many of those suckers had gone down my throat, I thought, a little too late. It didn't taste as bad as it looked or smelled, though. I waited for a few minutes to see if I would die or start throwing up, but nothing happened. I joined my brother and sisters in bouncing on a discarded conveyer belt, waiting for them to wonder why my face had turned green, but they said nothing. I didn't get sick and eventually forgot about it. Weeks later Granny was telling a story about how some kid had died from drinking bad water and warned us never to drink from the pond. "I drank from the pond," I said.

"When?" she asked.

"When I was little kid," I lied.

"Well, the pond may not have been as bad as it is now. That water out there now would probably kill you in a few seconds."

"OK," I said quietly.

For years after I was sure some rare, unexplainable malady would befall me when I least expected it, and on my deathbed I would whisper to my crying Granny about the pond water I drank, finally confessing my deepest secret.

On the shores of the pond, we built a fort made from grimy old boards and pieces of metal scavenged from about the yard. It was only large enough to house a couple of dogs but we were convinced it would pass as a real home. Derick, three years old at the time, suggested we "sell it to a bunch of hippies for $1,000." In an attempt to help his big sisters with the project, Derick grabbed a hammer and handfuls of four-inch nails out of "the shop," Duckels Construction's work garage. When no one else was around, he climbed onto the roof of our magnificent home of junk and pounded all the nails through. We could no longer enter the house without tearing up our scalp. Debi and I were angry for about an hour but them opted to destroy it to build a jump for our bicycles.

One time Derick decided to help Granny with the yard work by filling her lawnmower with water from the pond. Although there were probably enough petroleum chemicals in the pond to start something, the water destroyed the machine. Another time Debi convinced Derick—who was obviously too young to comprehend that advanced life forms couldn't possibly survive in that sludge— that she caught a fish from the pond. I don't know where she got the fish to show him, but to this day Derick is convinced she caught one, and we just laugh at him.

Occasionally our cousins, Chuckie and Sean, would visit Granny and Grampa. Dad's sister, Mary Ann, and her husband Chuck had moved away from Colorado so we didn't get to see them often. I got so excited to see them because I thought they were the grooviest people in the world. Unlike the country people who stayed in Steamboat, this family was cool. Chuckie and Sean were allowed to grow their hair out like the boys on the Brady Bunch, and Aunt Mary Ann looked right out of a 60's beach movie. Uncle Chuck grew a mustache, and even a beard for a while!

We played the usual construction yard games with the cousins. Climb on equipment, hide and seek in the equipment, throw rocks at the equipment, throw rocks in the bushes, throw rocks in the pond, run around the pond, push each other in the pond, get mad at being pushed in the pond and go tell Granny. I liked Chuckie and Sean a whole lot, and I do remember admiring their hair, and begging Dad to let Derick grow out his crew cut to be like them. It didn't do any good.

I remember thinking Aunt Mary Ann was as beautiful as an angel. She had very blond hair and a cute figure, and she'd look down a lot, like Princess Diana, because she was shy—as quiet as Dad! I'd stare at her sometimes and she'd smile back. I didn't know her well back then because she was a grown-up and I was kid, and they weren't around much. But I enjoyed being with her just so I could stare at her loveliness.

Uncle Chuck was and still is the friendliest, smilingest guy around. He was a scientist, and unlike Mary Ann he was talkative. He would fill us in on interesting facts about wildlife and nature and such. Mostly we were enamored with his mustache and beard. Uncle Chuck was the only man in our circle of family and friends who had facial hair, and even though his personality was quite conventional we imagined that we had a real hippie in the family. His hair gave the impression that he was slightly dangerous, or at least out of the ordinary. I hoped that some of his individualist style would rub off on my family. It didn't.

In winter, when the bridge-building and road-grading of Duckels Construction gave way to snow-plowing, we kids spent our days indoors at Granny's, occupying ourselves with projects less manly than equipment-climbing, fort-building, and pond-drinking. Granny painted our nails, let us try different perfumes, and taught us how to be ladylike. (Don't bend over at the waist; bend at the knees.) Our bodies swollen with sugar and our Goodwill clothes stained with Orange Crush and Grapette, she'd read us articles about keeping slim and dressing in good taste. We included Derick, the only boy in Steamboat to consistently have his nails painted. (He quickly discarded the habit after he started school.)

Granny had the world's pinkest bathroom, and I dreamed someday I'd have a bathroom just like it, and I could walk into it in my flowing pink robes with my glowing pink cheeks and take a dump. As a girl I would spend an unusual amount of time on the pot—long finished with what I'd come for—gazing longingly at the pink tiles, pink shag carpet, pink lace shower curtain, pink sink and toilet, pink Kleenex cover, pink tooth brushes, pink toilet paper. When I was in that bathroom, I was a princess sitting on my throne. In Granny's bathroom I could escape my feelings of inadequacy and know that someday I'd live in this kind of luxury—the luxury I deserved.

In the years to come, I seemed to identify more with the prissy stuff Granny had taught us than with the construction business. My brother and sisters learned early to run equipment and would sometimes work as laborers in the summer for Dad, but I had no stamina when it came to digging ditches and cleaning up after construction sites. At age fourteen I began my first job as a hotel maid and ended up working in restaurants all through high school. Today I am the only member of my family who never worked in the construction trade.

Granny and Grampa devoted over 30 years to Duckels Construction. For milder weather when they got older—in the mid 1980's—they moved to the Fort Collins area. Even in retirement they never managed to slow their habits. Both worked harder than any people I know, even into their 80s. Grampa had six garages on a property in Kersey, Colorado because he wanted to keep busy building things. He pounded nails until his yard was jam-packed with garages. He stopped only because he had no more room. In her 80s Granny single-handedly moved fallen trees around on her property, and mowed her yard with one of those powerless hand-pushers.

Grampa's health declined in his last years. When he turned 85 I asked him, "What does it feel like to be 85, Grampa?" and he replied, "Oh, same as when you're 25 only you can't see, can't hear, can't walk." My devoted Grandmother tirelessly took care of him all by herself until his death at age 91. And she's still hanging in there.

Their Elk River property in Steamboat is still home to the now prestigious Duckels Construction, Inc., for many years the largest construction company in northwest

Colorado. With dozens of employees and jobs that earn several million dollars each, Grampa and Granny's legacy has blossomed. The yard is nicely organized with rows of new, costly earth-moving equipment and updated buildings and mechanic's shops. If you drive around Steamboat you'll find evidence around every corner (or right under your feet) of projects in which Duckels construction was involved. The famous ski jumps, Pearl, Dumont, and Bear lakes, dozens of bridges including the James Brown Soul Center of the Universe Bridge, the Catholic church I was brought up in, roads galore. Rarely is Duckels not involved in projects all over northwest Colorado, as well. Dad is in charge now, and my brother Derick may one day take over the company.

The stone house Granny and Grampa built together still stands to the right as you drive past the DUCKELS CONSTRUCTION, SINCE 1956 sign; its tin roof is a little rusted and the grass is usually too long. But it has worn well through more than a half-century of Steamboat weather, mechanic's grease, and rowdy kids.

I Do Not Eat Deer Meat

Ask Dori, Debi, Derick or Dana Duckels what they think of hunting and you will hear the same answer. We do not like it. None of us has any moral objections to it, and we kind of liked that our Dad did it, but our experience participating in the sport is not cherished. Dad and Grampa hunted each year for as many elk and deer as their licenses would permit, usually one of each animal per man. I remember being proud of Dad when he'd come home with his trophy. He would leave in the morning long before sunrise in freezing weather and come home in the evening with his slit-open animal tied to the top of the station wagon or lying in the back of his pickup. He would look cold and tired. He would smell like blood and his hair would be matted down from his dirty orange hunting cap. I thought it very masculine and kind of scary.

We did show interest in how big the rack was. The minute he got home we ran to the door asking, "How many points?" Dad was not a show off, so we never had dead animal heads on our walls, but he was known to come home with some good-looking antlers. He didn't show off his famous hunting wound, either, although we asked him all the time. Loris Werner, brother of our local skiing legend, Buddy, accidentally shot him in the arm with an arrow on a hunting trip, years before we were born. Now that was something anybody should want to show off!

Occasionally my siblings and I were asked to go hunting. I will tell of only one outing. They were all the same.

Dad never took more than two of us hunting at once. This particular trip was for jack-rabbit. Covered from head to toe in winter apparel and bright orange outerwear Dad, Derick, and I set out at 4:30 in the morning to one of Dad's secret hunting areas not far at all from town. Derick was 6 and I was 11. My bobbing head fought to stay up as the pickup rolled down the dirt road in the frosty dawn. When it was barely light enough to see, we parked and got out. Remembering that Dad was usually gone all day for hunting was a sickening shock. The cold was cruel the second we opened the pickup door. How did he last all day?

Our instructions were plain: "Be quiet and follow me." We walked silently in the shallow snow prints Dad made through sage brush and scrub oak; it was October and only a few inches had fallen so far. He moved stealthily along, his gun ready and his eyes scanning the surrounding hills. I couldn't have picked out a giant orange bear on that colorless morning, let alone a teeny gray rabbit who could hide in the bushes.

We were quiet and we followed.

My thoughts proceeded in a circle as we walked: I'm cold. How could he possibly see anything? This is boring. We can't even talk. I'm cold. How could he possibly see anything? This is boring. We can't even talk.

We were quiet and we followed.

Occasionally Dad would stop abruptly and say, "Shhh," even though we hadn't uttered a peep. He would scrutinize a distant hillside and whisper for us to stand perfectly still. We would. We'd peer in the direction he was looking and see nothing but scrubby hills. Then he'd start walking again.

We were quiet and we followed.

Eventually my contemplation would degenerate from a circle into a downward spiral: I'm freezing to death. No way will he ever find anything. I'm bored out of my skull. I'm going to scream if I can't talk. I'm freezing to death. No way will he ever find anything. I'm bored out of my skull. I'm going to scream if I can't talk.

We were quiet and we followed.

This went on for about an hour and a half. Suddenly, out of the icy silence, BOOM! Before we even had time to notice that Dad had seen something, he threw up his rifle, aimed a million miles away, and blew off some bunny's head.

"I got him," he said quietly. "Let's go get him."

Overjoyed that we could finally talk, we started firing questions at him. "How did you find him? How do you know you hit him? Where is he? I can't see anything. What are we going to do with him? Can we not be quiet anymore? I have to go to the bathroom."

Dad was quiet and modest as usual. He didn't think anything of sighting and successfully plugging a tiny fast-moving animal darting through bushes a quarter-mile away. (He answered no questions about bathrooms. We knew we could pull our pants down anywhere and anytime we wanted.)

I felt relieved that we were almost finished with our task until we started the dreaded journey down into a valley and back up a mountain to find that rabbit. It was remarkably farther than it looked. Again I doubted Dad. How did he think he was going to find that tiny little speck mixed in with all those bushes? Was he sure he even saw it from that distance? What if he had missed? We trudged on, asking questions that were mostly not answered.

Dad walked right to the spot where the rabbit was, picked it up and handed it to me. I was mortified.

"I'm not carrying it!" I said.

"You have to. I've got the gun and Derick's too little. Quit being a sissy."

"I'll carry the gun."

"No you won't."

With a look of distaste I took the rabbit's hind legs and held it out in front of me at arm's length with one hand. It was heavy and dripping blood. For about ten steps I held it away from my body and nose, but its weight was more than I could handle. I wrapped both hands around it.

Another twenty steps and I realized I couldn't carry it like that all the way back to the truck. I pulled the rabbit to my chest and tried not to care that blood was spilling on my shoes and the smell of fresh meat was right under my nose.

Halfway back to the truck I didn't care what it smelled like or how much blood got on me—it was heavy and my arms hurt. I hoisted it into my arms and clutched it like a newborn baby. I was so looking forward to getting back to the warm truck I stopped caring about the smelly rabbit.

As we approached the truck, my hunting-hating attitude softened. As long as I could thaw out my feet and get home right away I didn't mind it so much. But just as I started climbing into the front seat Dad said, "What are you doing? We have to gut it."

Hunting-hating returned with full force. Derick and I squatted nearby and watched steam rise out of the rabbit as Dad slit it open. He cut out the guts and threw them in the bushes. He grabbed an old rag out of the back of his truck and wiped his hands on it. Although I'd seen Dad gut animals many times, I never had an inkling of an aspiration to try it myself. Though when I watched I always did respect his lack of squeamishness and his knowledge of the process. His quickness showed a familiarity with the undertaking that revealed his past. He had been a real country boy.

After the rabbit had been cleaned, Dad laid it in the back of the truck and finally we got in the cab and cranked the heater. As we drove back over the dirt road we got hotter and the smell of blood from my clothes and Dad's hands got stronger. Outside snow was swirling; a storm was moving in. I was glad we got that rabbit before lunchtime.

All hunting trips were the same, no matter what the animal. It was always cold and quiet and boring and tiring. But that wasn't the end. Parts Two and Three of the hunting sport made it even worse: processing the meat and eating it.

Instead of opting for OK Locker, the commercial meat packer, to process our game, our family used the economy method—slaughtering and dividing up the meat in our miniscule kitchen at home in the Old House. For game bigger than a rabbit, the process started in the dining room— also tiny—where Dad laid a side of deer (or elk) against the wall. Mom had to move a garage sale painting to accommodate the six-foot-high smelly carcass. We had a family assembly line. Dad would cut hunks of meat off the animal and designate the title of the cut. Some cuts were given to the kid with the hand-grinder who would add fat and make burger meat. Other cuts were allocated to the steak kid who would wrap the cut in Saran Wrap and butcher paper, and use a Magic Marker to label it Steak. There was a stew kid and a jerky kid. Mom helped with every step of the process including filling every inch of the freezer with white paper packages, our food supply for the year.

To this day I do not eat deer meat. When people talk of the lovely venison they had at So-and-So fancy restaurant I nearly gag. After an entire childhood of deer and elk everything for every meal I have simply filled my quota for this lifetime. As an adult I can surely appreciate my parents desire to save money (they must have saved a ton) but it made a beef lover out of me.

I have little to say about fishing. My brother and sisters for some reason didn't mind it so much, but I disliked fishing as much as hunting. I could not grasp the concept of standing around, bored to death, looking and waiting for something to happen, all the while being eaten alive by mosquitoes. Looking and waiting for things is not fun. It's exactly like looking for your lost keys or waiting for a friend who's late—not fun! Then, when and if the desired result occurred, that is, catching a fish, you have to actually use your bare hands to kill an animal struggling for its life. Of course, the gutting procedure needs no further explanation. And after all that you have to eat the stuff. I have the same distaste for trout as I do for deer meat. We ate too much of it.

I wish I could say that I noticed the sublime beauty of roaring Rocky Mountain creeks and high-country streams meandering through banks of Indian Paintbrush and Columbines. I just didn't. I wanted to go home and paint my fingernails.

Now camping was a sport I could get into. Only on rare occasions would our family camp. We lived full-time in the outdoorsman's quintessential paradise; why would we need to pack up in a car and enjoy it down the road? But the lure of preparing for two days, gathering up four kids and all their junk, driving an overloaded station wagon a few miles out of town to unpack and gather wood, set up tents, and start preparing meals was so seductive my parents did actually venture forth once in a while. I do remember enjoying it tremendously. Dad would fish for our dinner (trout, yuck) while we kids explored in the woods and Mom worked around camp. Several times we camped up Seed House Road near the Mount Zirkle Wilderness Area. Not far from Steamboat, Zirkle is a rugged, breathtaking, Colorado mountain playground with rare wildlife, snowy peaks, and incredible back-country trails. But for us kids, rejoicing in nature was not near as entertaining as playing in the tent. We pretended we were at home, of course, and divided the tent into our bedrooms and fought over what space was whose. We brought pine cones in for fake food, sticks to beat each other with if our property was invaded, and wildflowers and grass to decorate.

Meals were outstanding because of the fascination of the fire, and besides, camping makes one very hungry. Even trout and deer burgers weren't as bad. But the pinnacle of camping enjoyment, the Holy Grail of outdoor pleasure, the Super Bowl of campfire cuisine was S'mores. All day we'd talk about them. We'd bug Mom (where are the S'mores—did you bring the stuff—when do we get them—can we have some for an afternoon snack?) until she threatened to throw the marshmallows in the creek. We'd inspect the ingredients every half hour to make sure they were OK. We'd kill ourselves trying to get the ideal stick from the woods and whittle it to be the perfect S'more Chef instrument. We'd wolf down our dinner so we could get to the S'mores quicker. And then, by the light of smoldering logs, while Mom played sad songs on her sweet ukulele and Dad sat still and quiet on a pulled-up log, we kids made a science of cramming burning hot black marshmallows between sheets of chocolate and graham crackers. Although the eating of it was painfully superb, creating the precise level of marshmallow burn on the chocolate at the accurate time to acquire the maximum melt degree into the graham cracker might have been even more tantalizing. We couldn't possibly stop until our nervous systems and bellies were so gorged with sugar we were confused, nauseous, and exhausted. The process was utterly satisfying.

Colorado mountain nights were cold, even in the summer. I don't remember ever being quite warm enough in the tent, and we never seemed to get rid of all the pebbles under our backs. Not much sleeping took place. I spent most of our camping nights gazing at complete and total blackness and listening to Debi, Derick and Dana breathe. I have not gone a night in my life without having to get up to wee-wee, so I kept the flashlight in my sleeping bag. Creeping out into the very cold, quiet night in bare feet to stick my naked bottom in the wet grass was not nearly as bad as imagining the hungry bear with fangs bigger than my head waiting in the nearby trees to eat my naked bottom. I heard every noise for a hundred miles and was sure that every rustle of a leaf or babble from the creek was the sound of my ultimate doom. I would sprint back to the tent and desperately zip the door with a frenzy, envisioning a pack of mean mountain lions clawing to get in.

Only when we'd go away from local, familiar places to camp would we find interest outside the tent. Camping trips to Utah afforded a vastly different landscape and climate, so foreign we couldn't help but be in awe and wonder. This was a place we said WOW about, and explored with gusto. The tent held no interest when we were in Utah.

Moab was then a sleepy, insignificant place with nothing but a few rundown stores and a handful of rickety houses. The only civilization available in the east part of the state, Moab was the outpost for both Arches and Canyonlands, the glorious National Parks that were our camping destination. We used Moab for gas and sundry supplies. The town was practically deserted and the parks hosted only a handful of sightseers then; the place has become an overgrown tourist spectacle, like Steamboat, in recent years.

Just seeing the strange stone bridge formations, astonishingly deep canyons, and brilliant colored layers of rock from the car was enough to be worth the trip. Unlike our rides in the car back home where we invariably ignored the scenery and cared only about harassing each other in the back seat, we were plastered to the car windows in Utah. And getting out of the car to climb around was thrilling. Compared to the Colorado mountain terrain we were so used to, Utah was wonderful and weird. The cloudless cobalt sky looked bluer against the red sandstone cliffs and formations; the warm desert air; the fresh smells of sage, juniper and pinion; the odd-shaped cacti and succulents confirmed we were in alien surroundings. We'd scream at each other to "come look at this!" every few seconds. I imagined from the moment I got out of the car that I was an exotic desert Bedouin princess (with a veil and shiny jewelry, of course) surveying my lands and waiting for my handsome horseman (with a turban, of course) to come riding through one of those big red arches. One of the other kids would ruin my fantasy by showing me how far they could jump off a boulder or how high they'd climbed up a rock pile. Then I'd immediately forget about turbans and see if I could jump or climb farther.

Around the campsite we'd play until it was too dark to see—finding unusual rocks (which were all over the place) collecting bizarre-shaped pieces of driftwood, rock climbing and even just staring at the natural splendor—and Mom would call us to dinner. While wolfing down hotdogs and S'mores, we'd complain that we wanted to move to Utah. She'd say, yeah, OK, sure, but we never did, of course.

Because our camping trips were infrequent and our obsession with playing in the tent was strong, Dad often set up the tent in our yard at home for weeks in the summer. We'd spend the night out there fairly often in groups of kids according to who was getting along with whom at the time. Rarely were all four of us out there at the same time, but it did happen. I was the wimp of the bunch. If I couldn't stand the cold for a couple of nights in a row I'd be inside from then on.

Our friendly animals insisted upon joining us. If we didn't let them in at first, they'd claw on the tent until we did. Although the cats loved us, they did not always like each other. Occasionally in the night they'd have an insane battle (typical of all cat fights) on Debi's head. For an unknown reason their screeching, scratching skirmishes always took place right on Debi's face and hair. In the midst of the cats' uncontrollably vicious and maniacal conflict, Debi would join in with terrified howling and batting of arms. She'd scream for help while the cats tangled her hair and shrieked in her ears wielding sharp claws and frightening hisses. Poor me, I had no intention of sticking my arms into that untidiness to rescue my sister. I surmised that interfering would just add to the chaos. I sat in the corner grimacing with any other sibling who happened to be with us that night. Eventually the furor would die down and Debi would emerge; a blubbering, red-faced, messy-haired casualty of war. The cats would retreat to either side of the tent, still hissing and prickly until we shooed them outside with our blankets. Debi would continue crying as she grabbed her pillow to go in for the night. Those of us left in the tent would try to sleep for a while, but never lasted long. The cats would start scratching to get in again, and we would know better than to acquiesce. We'd eventually seize our pillows in a huff and set out for the great indoors, too.

I witnessed only a few of the Debi's-Head-Cat-Fights firsthand. Much of the time I slept inside, due to the cold, so I would be wakened in my bed at night by the howls of Debi and the cats through the window. Whether she slept in the tent or outside in her sleeping bag under the stars, the cats were drawn to her cranium for their prize fights. With vehemence she communicated to us that the cat fights were extremely traumatizing, that she was completely and absolutely devastated by them (understandably). Yet she was the kid most likely to sleep outside. I was certainly mystified. If it happened to me once, I would never sleep outdoors for the rest of my life. I would have the cats exterminated. I would start an organization promoting friendly cat relations. I never understood how she could brave the situation more than once.

People come from all over to hunt, fish, and camp in Steamboat. I don't blame them. I look back at how blind I was to the natural magnificence of my hometown, but I don't regret it. I found pleasure in what captivated me at the time. When I return home now I am awed by my native land and soak it in like I've never seen it before, but there is a familiarity so deep in the smells and sights and noises it feels as if I've never left. When I was a kid I couldn't help but absorb it all, even if it was only the backdrop for what I thought was important: laughing with my siblings, dreaming about being somewhere else, or living out my obligatory daily life. Although fishing and hunting never caught on for me, I am glad Dad dragged me out in the wilds and exposed me to the beauty, power (and discomforts) of nature, to primitive and ancient ways of getting food. And I'm happy that he demonstrating his self-sufficiency and connection to the Earth that is harder and harder to come by now. I still don't eat deer meat, but I don't mind telling stories about why not.

The Little Farts

The lifeguards at the town swimming pool called us something like The Little Farts. Only it was another word that started with an F. By the time I was age 12 I'd spent two thirds of my life at the pool and had caused enough trouble to be yelled at for just about everything you can do wrong at a pool, and was even kicked out a few times. Very little of my misconduct was acted out alone; Debi and sometimes Melanie Sprengle would be yelled at or kicked out with me. But we didn't start out being bad. We were good kids until Mom stopped coming to the pool with us.

In our early years, we frequented the pool because Mom worked there in the summertime, either as a lifeguard, swimming teacher, or gal behind the counter. She believed in the get-those-kids-underwater-when-they're-teeny-tiny-babies method of teaching, and taught her own kids to swim when we were a few months old. She taught many of the kids in town to swim before they could walk. I heard reports that she was strict. But those babies all learned how to swim well.

Mom taught beginners classes for a while, and then changed to teaching the advanced classes: the ones that taught water safety and perfecting strokes. I was thrilled that these classes involved the use of "Resusci-Annie," a life-size rubber lady in a blue polyester gym-suit on which the students practiced mouth-to-mouth resuscitation. Annie had corpse-white skin, and hair of a matted, sickly yellow color. Her thin lips stayed open to reveal a fakey pink tongue. When I was half the age of most of the advanced students, Mom required me to take the class and help her demonstrate on Annie. I am far too familiar with those lips and tongue. If you should happen to find yourself half-dead from breathing in water, you would definitely want me with you. I had to take the class over and over, almost until Mom no longer taught swimming lessons.

Bend down and listen for breathing.

Pinch the nose.

Pull the head back but not too far—just enough to straighten the air passage.

Take a deep breath.

Blow hard. Make sure your lips make a tight seal around her mouth.

Repeat.

Mom designated me as Annie's keeper. I would make sure plenty of kids were watching on the afternoons when I'd have to lift Annie out of the trunk where she lay folded in half, with her nose between her feet. I'd pretend to be bored as I threw her over my shoulder and carried her to the deep-end where Mom was bellowing at her students to get out of the water and come over quick. Most of Annie's body had to be inflated to look more lifelike. I'd look at my fingernails or tap on the cement as the foot pump filled her with air, and I filled with self-importance. I'd stand back and act uninterested as Mom explained the intricacies of bringing someone back to life. I'd heard it a million times. I knew all that stuff already. Resusci-Annie had a monitor built in her lungs that registered whether or not you were blowing hard enough to fill her lungs properly. It was not easy to get that needle up to the red zone, especially for a kid. When Mom motioned for me to come over and show them what to do, I knew that I'd make it look far too easy. I'd get down there and do my job without a word, and those big kids would think it was as simple as exhaling. And after they tried it themselves they'd look at me and whisper to each other. I knew they were talking about how amazing I was. I'd try not to smile. I passed the class years before kids my age took it. I felt quite valuable with my big blows and my personal friendship with Annie.

Alas, after a few summers of sucking face with Annie, she made me sick. Between each kid that practiced breathing into her, my Mom would wipe Annie's lips and mouth with rubbing alcohol. Every time I'd bend down and look into those foggy glass eyes with little scratches on them and pull back on her tangled, cheap hair I'd give her a dirty look. The smell and taste of alcohol on those cold lips eventually produced a gag reflex that inhibited my powers of driving enough air into her lungs. My glory days as the young prodigy who excelled at making out with the rubber woman came to an end.

Mom quit teaching swimming not long after. I was convinced it was because she didn't have me to boss around, but she said that the world of swimming was changing and the new ideas about swimming strokes were too hard to keep up with. She thought the old ways were best. Her sports interest moved to the softball fields, and she stopped coming to the pool except to lay out in the sun once in a while.

Mom made sure that we kept our family season pass at the pool, and that we milked it. Almost every day in the summer and on weekends in the dead of winter Mom dumped us off at the pool, usually from open to close. There was an Olympic-sized outdoor pool with water at a usual pool temperature, and a covered indoor pool with hot spring water. Summer at the pool was like in any other town, but winter turned the place into an entirely different experience.

In winter the outdoor pool was empty and closed. The indoor pool could be seen for miles—not its actual structure, but its billowing clouds of white steam rolling high into the frosty air. The leafless trees around the pool area were usually covered with a sparkling layer of white frost where water vapor had collected and immediately frozen. Not many of our classmates had year-round passes; the thought of donning a swimsuit and walking outdoors, across ice, to swim didn't appeal to most people when it was below zero much of the time. This left whole weekends of near-private swimming for the Duckels kids and the occasional hearty friend who joined us. Tourists came for short swims, but not in great numbers.

The indoor pool was housed in a modern A-frame building of dark wood and lots of glass. Its water was as hot as when it came out of the ground in the nearby Heart Springs—102 degrees. To get from the pool office—home of the locker rooms—to the indoor pool, one had to walk barefoot about 30 feet along an outdoor covered sidewalk. The path was almost always covered with ice, and if it was cold enough our feet would stick to it. Other times it would be slick and we'd cringe to watch the inexperienced tourists try to make their way slowly over it. The office gals poured salt on it regularly, but with all the warm, wet feet and dripping bathing suits passing over, it quickly iced up again.

In winter the indoor pool was ideal for hide-and-seek. The steam forbade you from seeing more than a few feet in front of your face. At night it was as if you were blind. We had to track each other by sound and touch, and hide-and-seek became a serious game of stealth, of hunter and prey, of daring and cunning, and (mostly) a good way to leave your brother or sister skulking around in the water, looking for you, while you went to the bathroom, took a sauna, and ate a snack.

"Where were you?" Derick asked one time when I ditched him in the fog for 20 minutes.

"What do you mean? I was looking for you."

"You were not. I swam all over the pool and you weren't here."

"What are you talking about? You must have just missed me. I was swimming all over the pool, too. I thought you were the one who left."

"I heard the door to the pool open twice. There's no one else here."

"Oh, didn't you see that man that came in here? He had a black mustache and blue swimming trunks. He was in here for a few minutes. That must be who you heard."

Derick was quiet, mulling over my lies and trying to decide if he should believe me. I don't think he did, but he didn't say anything. I think he stored those incidents away to use on me in later years.

There are only so many things that kids can do in a pool of hot water. Swimming laps, playing underwater screaming games, underwater foot races, floating around and looking at the ceiling, dunking each other, racing each other, playing Marco Polo (no need for closed eyes—the steam blindfolded us), standing on each other's shoulders and jumping off...after several hours we'd tire of the usual pastimes and flop lazily on the steps of the shallow end, our young minds stretching to invent more creative ways to pass the time.

The sauna, a small wooden hut situated about 30 feet from the indoor pool, would give us a few minutes of variety, but invariably an adult who was trying to relax and meditate would scold us for being disruptive. We'd get angry at Mr. Poopy Pants in the sauna and return via the packed snow path to the pool to concoct a plan for retaliation. We'd prepare detailed conversations, rehearse them, and casually return to the sauna to act them out. We considered our dialogues to be very sophisticated, and always involved a strategy to make us look like big shots.

"When did you get that swimming suit?" Debi would ask Melanie Sprengle.

"Yesterday. I bought about twenty suits yesterday."

"Where did you buy them?" I asked.

"I had my butler fly to France to get them."

"Really?" I said, "My butler was in France yesterday, too. I'm surprised they didn't run into each other. My butler was buying me a new diamond ring."

"What happened to your old one?" Debi asked.

"I didn't like it so I threw it in the garbage."

"Yeah. I can't count how many diamond rings I've thrown in the trash," Debi said. "I hate it when they don't shine right."

"Me, too," Melanie said.

We would receive no scolding from adults during our exchanges, but we'd watch the looks on their faces start with amusement, advance to eye-rolling, and eventually they'd close their eyes and pretend we weren't there. We could continue straight-faced as long as we could hold up to the heat of the sauna—maybe 20 minutes. Eventually we'd be red and sweaty and the scorched air would feel like it was burning our air pipes. We'd say something about needing to feed our pet gorilla. We'd fart as we walked out the door or emit a hellish scream about how cold it was, and run back to the pool. Once back in the water we'd laugh and congratulate whoever had performed the best, or come up with the best lies. Then we'd sit and stare and try to come up with a better idea.

We could always resort to rolling in the snow, but it was best done when the pool was populated with a good number of tourists. Showing off increased the pleasure of snow-rolling tenfold. Back in those days, a good number of tourists would be about eight.

We would position ourselves on opposite sides of the shallow-end and have a loud conversation across the pool so that all the tourists would be sure to hear.

"Hey Debi! Wanna go roll in the snow?"

"Nah! It's not cold enough!"

"Come on! I'm too hot!"

"All right, all right!"

The tourists would look our way. We'd wait until they had all migrated to our area with interest. We'd climb out of the pool feigning indifference, walk out the door, and pick a spot to snow-roll just outside the glass walls where our audience could see us well—if the steam cleared for a few seconds. We'd tiptoe across the ice outside and stand for a few agonizing minutes, waiting for the tourists to assemble along the edge of the pool. We'd pretend to be conversing casually, but would actually be saying things like, "Hi. How are you? My feet are going to turn black and fall off any minute."

"Oh really? That's nice. My butt-hole is freezing shut."

Steam would rise off our bodies like we were on fire.
"Wait for a good break in the steam so they can see."
"GO!"

We'd race for the snowbank, take a flying leap and roll and flop like dying fish. Snow clumps stuck in our hair and to our suits and slid off our steaming bodies.

Here's the thing: Snow-rolling hurts. A lot.

It feels like piercing stabs of fire needles. Your breath goes somewhere else, and to catch it again you have to remind yourself to. If the snow isn't perfectly soft powder, your skin is scratched by what feels like an icy crust. When it's new-fallen powder your body falls under all of it, and seems to cover you faster and with more pain.

We'd roll as long as we could for dramatic effect, and our show-off screams—halted and gasping from shock— entertained the crowd. When we could handle no more we'd race back to the pool while taking care not to slip on the ice, shrieking louder than before for the benefit of the spectators. The worst part was yet to come—jumping in the water. The first time we snow-rolled (not long after we could walk, perhaps) we found that the re-entry into the water was a sorry reward for our troubles. Instead of relief, you experience a few minutes of stabbing pain again, only this time the pricklers are cold, and seem to be more painful than the snow. After a howling splash into the water with wide-eyed gawkers surrounding us, we'd exaggerate the suffering of post-snow-rolling with noisy moaning and wailing.

Rarely would a tourist copy us. The process was distasteful enough to think about for most fair-weather tourists, and we helped to dissuade even those macho Texas men who thought they could stand up to anything. We imagined what these people were thinking about us as we thawed. Surely they considered us to be brave, daring, crazy, funny, and, high on the list, tough. But what we wanted them to see in us most is that we were home. This was our pool. This was our snow. We were used to this behavior, and it was no big deal to us. Besides, tourists were the very few people on the planet Earth who (we imagined) might actually look up to us. Kids! We needed to give them good reason to keep doing it.

I remember only a few local people who frequented the pool as much as we did. There were the Joneses—Carla and her mom—who swam laps all summer in the cold pool, lounged in the hot pool by winter and smiled *constantly*. And there was old Mr. Cladson (not his real name) who sat on the bench of the hot pool all day long. Every day he'd call us girls over individually. For years we were too young to understand that his gentle questions and soft arm stroking were more than just the friendliness of a nice old man. Once we were old enough to figure out he was lecherous, we answered his questions from a distance. If he started inching his way down the bench in our direction, we inched ourselves away from him. His behavior elicited nothing more than snickers among women older than 11, and as far as I know, no one ever did anything to stop him. For decades Mr. Cladson sat at the pool, caressing generation after generation of young swimmers. I heard only one story of Mr. Cladson doing anything different at the pool. He once brought Mrs. Cladson to the pool. Another man sat next to her to chat, and

Mr. Cladson got in a fistfight with him. It happened on the one day I didn't happen to be there.

Debi and I were in charge of Derick and Dana at the pool. Although we tended to avoid them much of time at home, little kids were actually worth having around at the swimming pool. They could be easily tossed, you could teach them tricks (like you would a dog), and several of our favorite pool games required the use of them, such as chicken fights and horse races. They were easily fooled into approaching tourists with questions we'd feed them.

"Excuse me sir, but could I borrow your swimming suit for a minute?"

"Ma'am, could you tell me which side of the pool is best to tinkle in?"

"Did you happen to see my goldfish swim by here?"

We'd watch the looks on the tourist's faces and dive underwater to laugh. Most of the time the tourist would start up a conversation with the little kids. Derick or Dana would swim back to us with serious faces, ready to report what their victim had said. They were too young to see what was so funny about it, but they knew they would be in good favor with their older siblings for what they did.

Derick had several incidents at the pool involving gum. Always in the mood for sugar, he procured it any way he could, including digging his hand into the pool ashtrays to get pre-chewed gum. I caught him more than once looking on the underside of the ice-covered benches outside, knowing good and well what he was looking for. One time Mom came to pick us up in the evening and as we drove away, heard Derick whimpering in the back of the car with one hand over his eye. As usual Debi and I had paid no attention to his hours of moaning at the pool.

"What's wrong?" Mom asked.

Derick pulled his hand off his eye and said, "A piece of gum got stuck in my eye." A gray and pink mass of goo had glued his lids shut.

"How the hell did that happen?"

"I was swimming, and it was floating in the water, and it just floated into my eye."

The car exploded with laughter. Mom was banging on the steering wheel with tears rolling down her face, and Debi and I were howling and prying back his hands to see it.

"It's not funny! I can't see!" Derick said as tears rolled out of his one good eye.

Mom had to pull over—not to try to help Derick, but to avoid careening off the road in her fit of laughter. We eventually made it home, and although Mom usually took care of gum removal from hair, she made Derick wait until Dad got home to tackle eye surgery. Removal of ticks and splinters were Dad's area of expertise, and this special case proved to be no great challenge to him. Derick lost many eyelashes and had to put up with the retelling of the story to everyone in town, but he did regain his sight.

While lolling around in the shallow end one day, having exhausted the usual list of bad behavior, Dana and I started a game that went on for years. Bored, I noticed various specks floating in the water and imagined what they might be. Skin? Ear wax? Fingernail dirt? We started a list that was added to every time we came to the pool—things that were most certainly floating around in the water. Belly button lint. Toe jam. Dingleberries. Dandruff. Pus. Scabs. Eyelashes. Tooth plaque. Boogers. Old makeup. Sweat. And tinkle, of course. Then we'd take a mouthful of the stuff and spit it on each other, screaming.

In winter the outdoor pool was mostly empty, but sometimes a few inches of water would accumulate from melting snow. Because no chemicals were used to treat the water, it would stagnate, and a greenish-black film would accumulate on the pool floor. When the pool attendants weren't looking—which was pretty much all the time—we would have running races on the slick, slimy, and smelly surface. Falling and becoming covered with the ugly stuff was the best part and eventually the race would turn into a slime-rolling extravaganza. We could have partaken in this original sport all day if it weren't for the unheated water and air.

We got caught more than a few times running back for the indoor pool covered in black germs and were yelled at (loudly) to go shower off before we got in the pool. The attendant would lecture us with disgust once we got cleaned up, and try to make us feel low and revolting. It didn't work even slightly. We were convinced anyone who would ever try slime races would be instantly hooked, and the only ones who didn't like it, hadn't tried it.

I think we eventually started causing more trouble simply because we ran out of other stuff to do. After all the games, snow-rolling, slime-racing, and tourist-taunting, our creativity eventually had to venture into new realms to maintain our sanity. Ten to twelve hours of 102-degree water, blinding steam, and siblings who lived to mastermind schemes could produce nothing but evil.

The cardinal rule of the Steamboat Health and Recreation Association (the pool's long-winded title then) was to never, never, ever swim in the Heart Spring. I'm not sure why this rule was strictly enforced; the spring is open to all swimmers now. This heart-shaped pool was built around the spring in 1922, and from this quaint, natural-looking formation, our big pools got their water. It lay over near the edge of the pool's property, and I don't believe I even took the time to go see the beautiful spring until I'd been coming to the pool for years, simply because I considered it to be useless if we wouldn't do something in or to it. When I finally walked over to see the crystal waters bubbling like champagne from under craggy rocks, I wondered how I could have gone so long without checking it out. I was convinced by the looks of it that it was scalding, because the bubbles made it look like it was boiling.

I never considered getting in the Heart Spring until one boring day, after all the games had been played and tricks pulled. Melanie Sprengle told Debi and me to follow her. We walked back through knee-deep snow in our dripping suits to the spring and admired it until, without warning, Melanie jumped in. I froze with horror, convinced that she'd boil alive. When she came up for air, laughing like a crazy woman, I was even more worried we'd get caught.

"Come on in," she yelled.

"Would you shut up? They're going to hear us!" I said.

Debi jumped in with a shout.

"You dumb-heads! I'm getting out of here."

I turned to go, but first asked, "How hot is it?"

"Same as the indoor pool. Come on in."

I climbed slowly in. It felt just like the indoor pool, but very different because I could see the rocky surface below, and because I was petrified that we'd be spotted. It felt free and wild. We dog-paddled around for a while, giggling and nervous. Just as we were climbing out, an attendant came in view.

"Get out of there now!" she said, so loud I fell back in the water.

"What the hell are you guys doing in there?"

We climbed out, trembling, dripping, and steaming.

"You are all three out of here! Get your towels and get out. Call your parents now and tell them to get you!"

We did as we were told, red-faced and guilty. We called Mom from the pay phone, saying that we weren't feeling well, which usually wasn't a good enough excuse, but we told her we were throwing up all over the place. She believed us when she picked us up because our faces were pretty green, and we didn't speak a word. Little Derick and Dana got in the back of the station wagon; we were relieved that they hadn't witnessed our criminal episode—they would never have let us get away with it.

"Why do we have to go home early? When did you guys get sick? You weren't sick a while ago. I was having fun," they said from the far reaches of the back of the car.

"Shut up! They're sick," Mom said.

The pool attendants didn't expect we could do much worse than swimming in the Heart Spring, but we proved them wrong.

We had never thrown snowballs because it was highly illegal in Steamboat (a hard-packed snowball could theoretically put an eye out), and the sight of a child dipping a hand into snow would produce riotous shouts from authority figures. So we figured out a brilliant plan to throw snowballs without getting caught. The snow banks surrounding the pool were easy to see, but no one would think to look on the roof! In our wet swimsuits we climbed a high snowbank near the roof and with a leg-up from Melanie, Debi and I stepped into the fluffy, untouched snow on the wood-shingles. Obviously it was cold, so we wasted no time in packing snowballs and pelting Melanie with them. She hid under the eaves and shouted that she'd alert us when to get ready for unsuspecting tourists. No more than a minute later we had the chance to assault a cute family of four, all fresh out of the dressing room in their dry suits and marveling at the icy walk to the pool. We made sure not to pack the snowballs too hard, and it wasn't easy with wet hands. Like expert snipers, we fired at our targets with no sympathy and plenty of accuracy. Snow exploded on their heads and shoulders, and they yelped. We thought they couldn't see us when we dived into the snow, but we were highly visible. They tiptoed back into the office and 30 seconds later the attendant came out.

She was used to kicking us out by now. Her gesture was simple and unmistakable, like an umpire calling an out. She tilted back her thumb, throwing it over her shoulder and yelled, "You're out of here! And you're not coming back for a week!"

She yelled all kinds of stuff about danger and childishness and poor tourists as we jumped into the snow below and trudged off to the locker room. We weren't near as timid as before. Getting kicked out was sort of cool now.

We didn't call Mom for a ride. Picking us up early twice in one winter would have aroused too much suspicion. We gathered up Derick and Dana and walked next door to Safeway, which is now the Post Office, where we loitered for three hours. In a small town in the 70's it wasn't the least bit unusual for four kids without parents to hang out in a grocery store all afternoon. We played hide and seek (a perfect game for a grocery store), sat and read magazines, and looked longingly at the candy. I bought just enough to bribe Derick and Dana to keep their mouths shut. At dinnertime we called Mom from the payphone and ran back over to the pool for our ride.

"Why is your hair dry?" she asked when she pulled up.

"We used the blow-dryers," we all suspiciously answered at once, eager to have a chance to use one of the lies we'd rehearsed. She didn't notice a thing.

I was in high school when I heard about our former title: The Little Farts. As a teenager I went to the pool only to lie on my towel and deep-fry in the high-altitude sun. The attendant that had yelled at us and kicked us out years earlier was in her late twenties by now and had come to like Debi and me because we'd outgrown our immature days. After all, she was like a nanny to us for years. She sat on her towel next to me one day; our charcoal tans matched.

"How long did you call us that?"

"Years."

"Were we that bad?"

"Yep."

"Didn't you think we were kind of clever, the stuff we thought up?"

"We called you Little Farts."

"Yeah, but didn't you kind of appreciate how goofy we were?"

"Nope."

"Do you think it's funny now?"

"I think the Little Farts name is."

"Yeah, me too."

The Big City

Several times a year we traveled to Denver to see Mom's family and do big-city things. In 1973, when the Eisenhower Tunnel was completed, Interstate 70 became a safe route over the mountains from Steamboat. Before that the route to Denver followed one road, US 40. Lincoln Avenue, our town's main street, lead out of town, meandered over the Rockies, and eventually became Colfax Avenue in downtown Denver. Never more than a two-lane highway with almost no shoulder, US 40 wound its way up and over two incredibly gorgeous high-country passes—Rabbit Ears and Berthoud. The last stretch of the journey followed the edge of a roaring creek at the bottom of a deep, rocky canyon. No one would disagree that it was breathtaking. As a kid I thought the four-hour ride was a bore, and I dreaded the journey because I almost always got car-sick.

Our family drove an older station wagon; a '54 Chevy took us through the 1960s. Our old car always managed to have just enough wrong with it that it would still run, but be very uncomfortable. It never failed that winter trips to Denver would be lacking one or more of the following conveniences: heat, defrost, or windshield wipers. Rabbit Ears Pass is 9, 426 feet at its highest, and parts of Berthoud Pass go above timberline, at 11,307 feet above sea level. Berthoud is cold even on the Fourth of July.

The passes, particularly Berthoud, periodically became impassable in winter. For up to a week Steamboat was essentially shut off from the bigger outside world. During these times, newspapers, gas, and food were not delivered from the big city. If our sense of isolation was acute during normal times, closing the pass accentuated the awareness exponentially. The idea that we physically could not leave our town was both humbling and exhilarating. On one hand it smacked of doing prison time, but there was also a feeling of being special, of being trapped together in an emergency situation. As a kid I could revel in the excitement. I wasn't inconvenienced with adult responsibilities and plans that go awry in crisis situations. I got to say, with great importance, "We're snowed in. The Pass is closed." If we'd planned a trip to Denver we'd have to cancel and wait until Berthoud reopened.

For the trip over the mountains, Mom and Dad devised techniques for dealing with our handicapped automobile that educated the whole family on how to handle ourselves in emergency blizzard or super-freezing conditions. Mom would dress her four kids in long johns, three layers of sweaters and socks, parkas, hats, scarves, mittens, and lined boots. We were skinny kids, but after being entombed in all that paraphernalia we could barely close the doors on either side of the back seat. Mom would toss a pile of blankets on us and tell us not to complain.

Without defrost, and with six people in the car, the windows would cloud up easily and quickly. If our windshield wipers did work, which was infrequent, they were too wimpy to keep the view clear. The only solution was to drive with the windows open. No talking was possible with blasting arctic winds screaming through the car. Even if we could hear each other, the nasty cold took our breath away. We shivered and winced.   It solved the problem of kids fighting or making noise in the backseat on a long trip. We huddled together with our heads down, sometimes under the blankets, and waited for it to be over. Mom had told us not to complain, and we didn't.

When it snowed on trips to Denver, visibility was often nearly zero. Mom was always amazed at Dad's ability to see in a snowstorm. From our perspective in the backseat we saw nothing but white flying specks. No road, no roadside—nothing but car and white. Dad managed to drive at his usual unhurried pace, humming leisurely as if he were on a dry road in the sunshine. He'd had a lifetime of navigating snow, and his eyes seemed to have developed X-ray vision in whiteouts. With the windows down, our backseat blanket became coated with snow. If inspired by a moment of playfulness, one of us would try to make a snowball or eat some of it, but we quickly retreated back to huddling and wincing.

A little less traumatic were the trips when only the heater was broken. Because we could keep the windows up we could actually hear each other speak, although our vigor was severely lacking. With stuttering speech we'd make a comment or two.

"Th-the-the snowbanks are higher than the car this year."

"Th-th-they're always higher than the car."

"One t-t-time they weren't."

"Sh-sh-shut up. I'm cold."

Later, as we descended the last stretch down to the front-range and saw the vast expanse of city below, temperatures increased abruptly, snow diminished entirely, and our morale swelled significantly. The thrill of going to Denver was boosted even higher by the reminder that we would be considerably less cold for a few days. Denver seemed to us a balmy place with year-round summer—a tropical paradise. We soaked it up, never for a moment allowing our minds to dwell on the dreaded trip back.

Mom's relatives were first on our Denver to-do list.

Though her real name was Francis, we called mom's mother Ahvee. Her nickname came about when I was tiny. I tried to say I love you, but it came out Ahvee. My grandmother hated the idea of being old enough to be called Grandmother, so decided to take my little word for her grandma name. Soon most people were referring to her as Ahvee.

She rented a small enchanting home, the carriage house of a huge estate. Occasionally the owners of the main house would invite us to stroll in their glorious gardens. They were so lovely they remain in my mind one of the most beautiful places I have ever been. The main house was like a European villa, and the gardens boasted a live-in gardener who tended the grounds. There were fountains, birdbaths, stone walls and walkways, hedges trimmed into shapes, and flowers, flowers, flowers. I was astounded at the beauty. When I hear the words Garden of Eden, that's what I picture.

The fancy carriage house suited elegant Ahvee. She had been a fashion model in her younger days—a six-foot, slender, black-haired, brown-eyed beauty. The word cute would be the exact opposite of Ahvee, in both looks and temperament. The first time I saw a movie with Marlena Dietrich I immediately remarked how much she reminded me of Ahvee. She read Vogue magazine, loved fine art (even modern and abstract), went to the symphony and the ballet, and wore furs. She read books insatiably and was informed about politics and all sorts of current issues. She did Yoga and studied all kinds of Eastern philosophies. She knew the use of all five forks at a stately dinner table.

        While her interests were cultured and refined, her behavior was sometimes not. She had strong opinions and spoke her mind. I think she might have prided herself on being a maverick and shocking people, so frequently things came out of her mouth that would not be considered grandmotherly. Her favorite joke (that she shared with me at a young age) included the F word and a reference to homosexuals. I remember riding in her Cadillac on the freeway in Denver and hearing her say, "I wish I had a tank so I could squash all these others cars." She disapproved of anything she deemed vulgar, and would voice her distaste stridently in public, careless of who she might offend. In the checkout line she'd loudly relay her thoughts about anything and anyone, including political or religious views, the attire or complexion of others nearby, the outlandish prices of food, and, to my horror, the regularity of her grandchildren's bowel movements. During movies she was at her noisiest. She would nearly shout her opinions about characters and plot, and her gasps and laughter could be heard throughout the theater. If she was disgusted about something she emitted a signature growl that involved a bit of hissing and statements like, "Oh how vulgar." If she liked something, her one and only saying, always sent off dramatically and drawn out, was, "Isn't that precious." Our family became excellent imitators of the two sayings.

I don't know why she was so fixated on poop. She rarely asked about our health except in regards to regularity. "Did you have a BM this morning? How was it? We might need to get you eating more bran." Mom had never taught us to worry about our health, that only if something was terribly wrong (as in a severed artery or being in a coma) would one's health demand attention. So we listened to Ahvee's BM talk with wonder and bemusement. We learned to head it off at the first question with, "I'm fine. My poop is fine. I went today and it was fine. Just exactly like you like it."

What I loved most about Ahvee was that she liked to sit and talk with me. She'd ask questions about my likes and dislikes, and although she could be quite judgmental about the answers, she made me feel important just because she asked and listened. She loved to tell stories about her younger days when she was beautiful. With starry eyes she'd recount the tale of her old beau, Franklin Something the Third, with the shiny red convertible, the gowns she used to have in her closet and what they were made of, society balls and movie premieres.

Of all my parent's children, I was the most interested in refinement. Ahvee knew she had a captive audience with me and educated me about art, literature, fashion, music, gourmet food, the theatre, and generally being snooty. I couldn't calculate how much her cultural education impacted my life, except to say that I loved it and set off after high school to pursue a life in the arts. Her contribution might have been large.

My descriptions of Ahvee might lead one to believe that she was financially well-off. She certainly was not. I asked Mom where she got all her money, and I was told that their family was never wealthy. At one time, when my grandfather was alive Ahvee lived a reasonably comfortable life. He was an architect, but didn't have his own firm. Mom thought that perhaps Ahvee had been mesmerized by the lifestyle of Franklin Something the Third during their brief relationship, and she lived the rest of her life imitating the rich and snobbish.

She and "Pop," my grandfather, lived in the house on Albion until he died of a heart attack when Ahvee was in her late 50s. After he died she sold the home and used the money to move into the fancy carriage house and buy expensive antiques to fill it. She gambled away the rest, hoping to pick the winning horse or dog at the track that would make her as rich as she pretended to be.

By the time I was old enough to observe and remember things, Ahvee's champagne tastes had outrun her beer budget. I experienced Ahvee after the fall of her glory, when her gorgeous antiques were faded and worn and her omelets employed margarine instead of butter. She neglected to clean up her ashtrays, and cigarette butts lay strewn about her marble coffee table. Wine stains tainted her white carpet, and her huge medieval tapestry had a fascinating brown blotch covering the Virgin Mary's arm and half of baby Jesus. She dressed in polyester suits and costume jewelry from rummage sales, but still managed to make them look striking. Of course she still had her furs, but they stunk a little and had holes under the arms. I know it was torture for her not to keep up the luxuries she'd loved.

What Ahvee didn't talk about was her childhood. From Mom I learned that Ahvee's early years could be summed up as a nightmare, but no one was quite sure what exactly happened. I asked Ahvee about it only once, and her whole being went dark. I quickly changed the subject, and she gladly went along. The story I put together for myself was that she surrounded herself with glamour to forget about her tragic childhood, but could only keep the demons at bay for so long. As her beauty and money faded, so did her illusion of happiness. I felt sad for her as I got older. She smoked and drank too much, frequently expressed her revulsion for all things vulgar (a long list), and could easily be described as paranoid. She always seemed to me a little haunted.

Visiting Bink, my mom's brother was also on our Denver list. Tall, thin, and attractive like his mother, Bink carried on her looks, but not her personality. He was down-to-Earth and jovial. The only grown-up who would play with the kids, he rode us on his back, played chase, and was always thinking of games for us. He, Aunt Mary, and our cousin Tania seemed to be a Normal Family. They had normal jobs, lived in a normal house and, most importantly, when interacting with others, seemed to be somewhat levelheaded and pleasant. Our house was full of noisy kids, my Mom's colorful language, and odd happenings at all hours. I always enjoyed being around Bink and family, but never stopped to notice how exceptional it was to be in such a comfortable, stable environment. I regret that I never fully appreciated the magnitude of how unusual they were. I can easily say that I had some seriously fun times at their place— playing games, having big holiday dinners, singing songs, and just sitting around talking—being normal.

Aside from visiting relatives, there was a short list of extra activities that we kids begged to do each time we went to Denver.

It was very important that we eat at McDonald's. Steamboat had no chain stores until I left home for college, and local restaurants and stores were, for the most part, expensive and limited. Ironically, for us there was something exotic about eating food or buying clothes that seemed to most people, and eventually came to seem even to us, boringly uniform and consistent. Knowing that a whole nation of people were eating the same burger or wearing the same shirt made us feel less isolated, less like hicks. It was exciting to participate in a worldwide phenomenon. I would marvel with exhilaration at the *10 million sold* sign on the golden arches, and feel satisfied to be contributing to the growing number on the sign.

As for the food at McDonald's, nothing could have made us happier than a burger made from actual beef. After our constant deer and elk diet, eating beef produced a temporary family euphoria, whereby we sat smiling dreamily together at our cramped McDonald's table, like the silly, cheerful people in commercials. I marveled at the particular flavor only McDonald's could bring to a burger and fries. It was mushier, flatter, and blander than the school lunch hamburgers—all good qualities to me at the time. Each member of the family was required to keep his or her individual food budget to under a dollar when we ate there, and we had no trouble accommodating the restriction. Our family of six ate for under six bucks.

After eating at McDonald's we begged to see the fancy stores, especially the ones downtown. They were so extraordinarily unlike the ones in Steamboat. Harwig's, Steamboat's local tack store, had been around since the 1880s. Creaking over worn, wide-plank floors we would meander around the saddles on sawhorses and run our hands through the leather bridles and halters, taking in the strong smell of leather. They kept Harwig's hot, and on freezing snowy days we'd duck in just to get warm. The Boggs, good friends of ours, owned Boggs Hardware, a pleasant place with friendly service and skinny aisles. FM Light and Sons sold jeans and cowboy-wear, and we'd spend hours trying on cowboy hats in the mirror. We ordered sodas and bought trinkets from Lyons Drug, which to this day sells old-fashioned sodas from their fountains.

I certainly didn't appreciate our Ma and Pa outfits back in Steamboat for their character and uniqueness. We'd seen them everyday, had been there a million times! They were just places where we got stuff or hung out. They were overly-familiar and outdated compared to the commercial extravaganza Denver had to offer.

May D and F Downtown, one of Denver's finest department stores, exemplified the pinnacle of dazzling glamour and elegance. (It might compare to the Bloomingdale's of today.) So dissimilar to our rural hometown shops, May D and F was like a walk through a magical fairyland. I'd marvel at the delicate features of the mannequins and their groovy outfits, dreaming of being a lovely lady in a palatial home just like May D and F. We'd walk reverently by the jewelry counters, pressing our awestruck faces against the glass. I'd have to be scolded for trying, always, to lie on one of the pristine mattresses. I was so captivated at May D and F that I'd nearly want to die when it was time to leave. No grown-up could have ever imagined how long I could have stayed there and just walked around and dreamed. Everything I looked at was transformed in my mind into my future fantasy life.

At Christmas we would plead and pester relentlessly until our beleaguered parents would take us downtown at night to see the lights. The May D and F windows were a statewide attraction and crowds pressed against each other to see the moving Santas and sparkling festive scenes. The Civic Center was (and still is) a spectacle of crazy, lit-up magnificence, and we gawked at it until our eyes were tired.

The lure of futuristic, shiny city stuff was a thrill, to be sure. But there was something even more exotic and fascinating about going to Denver.

We demanded that our parents take us to see black people. I will explain our seemingly backwards and bigoted mentality by relaying that we had only one African-American family in Steamboat, but my family almost never saw them. We saw black people on TV occasionally, but seeing people of different races in person was completely foreign to us. I couldn't have had a single thought of hating or judging a person for his or her skin color; I had never spoken with anyone who wasn't white. On rare occasions my Dad, after being ruthlessly harassed for hours, would give in and drive us though a predominantly black neighborhood. We would stare out the car windows to get a glimpse of the innocent people going about their lives.

"Hey, look! There's some playing in the yard!"

"I just saw one walking into his house!"

"Hey Dad. What do they do?"

"Oh, same things we do."

"Do they drive to our neighborhoods and look at us?"

"No, I don't think so."

"If they did I would do a dance for them in the yard."

"Oh yeah? I'd lift up my shirt and show them my white belly."

These were the conversations we had; I still remember as if it were yesterday how interesting and out-of-the-ordinary it was, and how excited and satisfied we'd be after these outings. I think Dad secretly kind of liked it, too, because he had also grown up in lily-white Steamboat.

The other ignorant pastime we loved was going down to Larimer Street to see the bums, as we then called homeless people. Again, we had not one homeless person in our cold little town, and the thought of homelessness was absolutely shocking and inconceivable to us. Every trip to Denver we would, as usual, beg Dad to drive us around looking for bums. Poor Dad thought our interest was funny, and occasionally would comply. We'd go at night for a better chance to see more bums out and about. Dad would hum and we kids would slunk down so only our eyes peeped out the window, in case a mean bum should try to attack us. One of us would shout with glee when a bum was sighted.

"Look! He's lying down!"

"Slow down, Dad! We want to get a look at him!"

"I'm not slowing down."

"There's another one! He looks really sad."

No matter how many bums we saw we'd ask Dad endless questions about them.
Why don't they get a home? What do they do when it's cold? What do they eat? Do they play sports? Where are their parents? Can I touch one? Dad gave the same answers, which were always short and with little explanation. So we kept asking. No amount of questions could quell our curiosity about something so foreign.

One cool summer Denver morning we were roused very early by Uncle Bink. He insisted we come quick, so we hustled out of our sleeping bags rubbing our eyes and straining to find the stairs out of the basement.

"There's a bum out in the ditch," he said. "Hurry! I thought you kids would like to see him." Bink lived in a suburban neighborhood with cute brick homes. "Look! There he is."

In the drainage culvert behind a chain link fence, a dark figure with a big blue coat skulked unsteadily toward us. We were so excited one would think we'd seen an albino giraffe.

"Let's go look at him!"

We sprinted up to the chain link fence and peered excitedly at the man. His big blue coat covered his face.

"He might be hungry! Let's get him some bread."

We ran back to the house and grabbed fistfuls of white bread as if we were going to feed birds in the park. We raced back to the fence and began shoving our rolled up bread balls through the holes in the chain link.

"Hey! We got some food for you!"

Suddenly the man lunged for us, yelling. We screamed and scampered away, terrified. Bink nearly fell over laughing and my Dad pulled the big blue coat from over his head.

Decades later, we still haven't heard the end of the teasing about the bum in the ditch.

A Snowplow for Every Street

To a person less than four feet tall, a fifteen-foot snow bank leaves an indelible impression. In years to come, this impression leads to the conviction that it snowed more when we were young than it does now. All Steamboat natives swear it snowed more when they were kids, and maybe it did. But no one can argue that it snowed a lot—way too much for some of us. We succumbed to certain facts: We were going to be cold most of the time; our parent's most time-consuming activity would be finding and warming up our car in the morning; we would not have snow days at school—that was for places without a snowplow for every street. Studded snow tires, chains, a powerful defrost button, and a blasting heater should be essential on all vehicles. (We were usually without all four, for some reason.) Just inside the front doors of our homes was a strewn-about labyrinth of boots, mittens, scarves, and parkas. No Steamboat citizen should need extra exercise from a fitness program. They get plenty from all the labor required just to get inside one's house. Shoveling and plowing ice and snow from driveways, sidewalks, decks, and roofs were often daily jobs that everyone was forced to perform, usually from November to sometime in April.

There were days on end when the temperature wouldn't rise above zero. Once when I was in fourth grade, our teacher, Mr. Austin, a newcomer to Steamboat, refused to leave his house and come to school, because he said it was too cold. Mr. Fitch, our principal, quoted Mr. Austin saying, "Humans are not meant to be outside in these temperatures." We native kids, who had walked up to a mile to the school or to a bus stop to get there, laughed and wondered how anyone could be such a wimp. It was 54 degrees below zero.

Although I was forced to live with it, I never got used to the cold. I could never understand how some of the other kids would wear a light jacket and no mittens or hat when it was below 10 degrees. I wore long johns under my clothes to school. The kids on the ski teams were even more of a mystery to me. They seemed to thrive on the snow and cold. The longer the winter lasted, the happier they were. It was as if they were from another planet. Or I was.

It usually started snowing in late October. One day you'd know from the dark gray sky and the crisp, energized air that the first real snowfall was on its way. Through the short weeks of brilliant fall in September and all of gray October I'd dread the oncoming winter, but for those anticipant few hours before the first flakes started, and while they swirled around my head, falling heavier by the minute, it felt like energy and exhilaration and peace.

I was always frustrated that almost every year we'd have a foot of snow on Halloween. Halloween was my one chance, once a year, to dress up like a beautiful princess or fairy and look graceful. Yet without fail my lovely costume would be completely covered with hats, boots, mittens, and parka.

"What are you supposed to be?" the treat-givers would ask from their doors.

"A fairy princess," I'd say sadly.

"Well let's see your costume."

I'd open up my parka and show a few inches of satiny material.

"Oh yeah. That costume must be real cute."

Stupid snow.

Unlike most places around the country, we in Steamboat were guaranteed snow at Christmas, and lots of it. We were the few lucky inhabitants of real-life Currier and Ives postcards, Norman Rockwell magazine covers, and cartoons of Rudolf and Frosty. Our houses were adorned with frost on the windowpanes and icicles that hung from the rooftops to the ground. People bundled in mountains of winter gear could be found skiing down the street to work, or trudging by snow-covered pine trees to school. Sledding, skiing, ice-skating, and snowmobiling weren't something we dreamed of in a song, they were mandatory if we wanted to have any fun. We didn't make snowmen; we made Amazon snow families, complete with grandparents, pets and, if we were ambitious, their house and car.

These things made Steamboat and snow bearable for that one week around Christmas. But even then the snow created extra demands on those trying to be festive. Outdoor Christmas lights strung on blue spruces would end up as barely visible lanterns poking through their suffocating coverlet of white. Of course they were more beautiful this way, but taking them down later required dexterity and craftiness. Baby Jesus in the occasional light-up nativity scene would spend the holidays prematurely entombed in snow unless his owner broomed him off twice a day.

My favorite custom, the Roving Christmas Tree, was an annual Rotary Club project. Middle-aged men drove around town in a flatbed truck with a shining Christmas Tree, a tremendously loud, tinny speaker playing Bing Crosby and Andy Williams, and a few poorly-costumed Santas running along side. The Sannies, as we called them, would give us a plastic bag full of candy and peanuts. If the Roving Christmas Tree would fail to make it down Spruce Street, we would all jump in our Kingwood Estate station wagon (with fake wood on the side), and drive up and down the streets with our window down listening for Nat King Cole or Frank Sinatra blaring into the night. It was usually below zero on these nights, but we barely noticed our frozenness in all the excitement. With the ferocity of a wild animal, one of us would shout "there it is" as soon as the tip of the Roving Christmas Tree poked its crooked star around a street corner. Before Dad could finish pulling the car against a snowbank on the side of the road, we would be surrounded by two or three Sannies, all clamoring to give us treats. We'd pour out of the car with angelic looks on our faces—proving that we were nice, not naughty—and answer the obligatory Sannie questions: Have you been good? What do you want for Christmas? It's cold out here isn't it? We had to yell our answers to be heard over the earsplitting loudspeaker carols. I'd receive my bag of delights and then gaze dreamily at Sannie for a few seconds, taking in his face, knowing I wouldn't see him again for another year. Then I'd squeal a thank you and race back to the car for warmth.

Back in the car, as we fondled our candy like baby kittens, we would ask Dad why the Roving Christmas Tree Sannies always had black eyebrows or falling mustaches, and he answered that they were only Santa's helpers, not the real thing.

The coldest I have ever been (and I have been cold many, many times) was one Christmas when my Mom and I went with the Wilhelms into the forest to cut down Christmas trees for us and several friends. We started out at Patsy and Willy's modest home in Elk River Estates (one of Steamboat's first subdivisions) where we saddled our horses and laughed and drank hot cider. Our breath was visible as usual, and I had that winter wonderland feeling that accompanied any outdoor Christmas festivity. Kim Wilhelm (my friend since early childhood) and I had to feed the chickens before we left, but other than that, it was our day to enjoy ourselves.

We headed into the forest with our license to cut Christmas trees. I was starting to get cold from the start. On horseback, with no movement in my limbs and no exercise to keep my body warm, my poor little hands and feet began turning frosty, and with hours ahead of us. Our horses trudged through an unbroken path of belly-deep snow; the spruce and pine trees around us were weighed down under clumps of white; the air smelled of crisp pine. At first Kim and I sang kiddie Christmas carols such as "You Better Watch Out" and "Frosty the Snowman," while I sporadically mentioned that it sure was cold. Kim and I pulled our horses off the deep path and fell to the back of the line to giggle behind the grown-ups for a while, whispering about whose horse had the fattest butt or about that chicken back in the hen house who had all the feathers picked off her butt. Butts are funny when you're eight years old.

As time ticked on, I began to hurt. I tried all the freeze remedies including blowing hot air into my mittens, pulling all my fingers into a ball, putting them against my belly, curling up my toes, and thinking about other things. An hour into the trip I was nearly crying, and we hadn't found a single tree.

Kim was much tougher than me, being a real cowgirl and all. She was cold, but was of the country opinion that whining was not acceptable behavior for anyone, even little girls. I started yelling up to Patsy and Mom at the front of the line, "That tree looks perfect. What's wrong with that one? It's not too big. You keep passing up good trees. We'll never find good ones if we keep riding this far," and so forth. Kim joined in, since it wasn't official whining; it was merely helping with the Christmas tree selection. Our parents told us to shut-up, that we weren't helping matters any.

Eventually we found trees. Patsy, my mom, and some other guy chopped them down, hooked them to the packhorses to drag, and turned us all around. By then I was positive I had frostbite and would lose both hands and both feet. I whimpered and moaned all the way back to Elk River, my extremities numb and throbbing. Our teacher in school had recently read us a story about a stupid man in Alaska who froze to death, and I was sure my time was coming, just like him. I imagined that any minute I would get that warm, tired feeling that meant I was dying. It never came. I remained frozen and miserable until the Wilhelm's roof became visible over the ridge. At that point, Kim, who hadn't spoken in an hour, created a plan for how we'd get warm once we got inside. We'd fill the bathtub with hot water and sit in it overnight.

We reached the house after dark. Kim and I dismounted and sprinted in the house. My feet were so numb I felt like I was running on stumps. We fumbled awkwardly to lock ourselves in the bathroom and began filling the tub with scalding water, while we clumsily undressed with our stiff, unmovable hands. Once naked we tested the water. "AAHH!"

"It's too hot," I said. "Let's empty the tub and get warm water instead."

"OK." Kim, a year older than me and much tougher, took the responsibility of doing the work. Once the tub was full again we tested the water.

"AAAHHH!"

"It hurts!" Kim said. "It needs to be colder." She emptied the tub again and filled it with barely warm water.

"AAAAHHHH!"

"Better go with cold," I said.

"We have to anyway. There's no hot water left."

When the tub was finally filled with cold water, we were able to slip in and begin to thaw. The adults had been too busy taking care of the horses to tell us about proper gradual-thawing procedure. The cold water, just a few degrees warmer than the outside cold, worked some warmth under our skin until we were able to feel alive again and move to slightly warmer water. It took hours of soaking and whimpering, but eventually we defrosted.

I still cringe when people mention the romance of cutting your own Christmas tree. I don't even like the thought of having a real Christmas tree in my house. My hands start going numb just looking at one. (Not really.)

The Wilhelms held the honorable position of supplying our family with the majority of our most romantic Christmas memories. Aside from the Over-Refrigerated Christmas Tree Hunt, we participated with Patsy and Kim in the most treasured of all Christmas pastimes, the sleigh ride. Each year Patsy, dressed in cowboy winter overalls and a plaid hat with earflaps, would hitch a couple workhorses to a hay-covered flatbed sleigh and drive them into town, 10 miles from Elk River Estates. Mom would have arranged for a group of our friends to meet the sleigh, usually at the Buddy Werner Memorial Library, and 20 of us would pile on for an evening of caroling and merriment. For the largest part of my growing up years, we'd use the snow-packed streets of Steamboat as our sleigh grounds, and when they heard the horses' jingle bells and our loud carols people would pop out their glowing front doors to watch us pass. We'd yell Merry Christmas and beam happily at each other. Kim and I would always ride on the back with our feet swinging off the end, and singing louder than anyone. Our favorite carol was *Blue Christmas*, and we'd sing it over and over in our imitation Elvis voices while the adults laughed at us.

Unfortunately, our idyllic scene couldn't last forever. When I was little, there was almost no traffic at night, even in town, so we had the run of every street. But one year, as we caroled past the little decorated shops on Lincoln Avenue, our Main Street, we were pulled over by a cop and told it was not safe to be sleigh-riding down the busiest street in town. There was not a soul in sight. With a little complaining we were relegated to all the other streets in town. A few years later, when tourism had increased enough to make the cops even more grouchy, we could no longer sleigh ride in town.

Patsy eventually began a winter sleigh ride company out near her house for tourists (one of her many ventures), and our old quixotic family-and-friends sleigh ride came to an end. My mom, who considered the Christmas sleigh ride to be as essential as milk, subsequently arranged sleigh rides with Pearly and Bonnie Green who lived far out 20 Mile Road. We'd drive a half hour to ride their sleigh around the snowy fields of their ranch, and although the scene was picturesque and charming, I bemoaned the fact that no one could hear our off-key carols except us. Sleigh riding in town had been one of those rare occasions when other people were insanely jealous of me—me! I had been one of the Steamboat Christmas Elite, one of the chosen few who waved happily from a dreamy winter scene, and all those poor suckers were jealous and bored, watching from their ordinary windows.

Every once in a while carolers—without a sleigh—would frolic past our house on Spruce, and we'd venture just out our door to listen, shivering in our slipper socks and thinking, hurry up and get it over with before we die. Dad would yell from behind his newspaper, "What's the matter? Ya born in a barn?" until we scampered back inside and rushed to the heater grate for warmth. We liked the *idea* of carolers, but opening the front door during a Steamboat winter is something you really want to do only in a emergency, or if you absolutely must leave the house, for work or food and such.

Later, when I was in high school, a few girlfriends and I once treated Steamboat to the ultimate caroling experience. We started at the house of Melanie Sprengle, which was uncharacteristically empty. Her parents and gobs of brothers and sisters were all away at a Christmas party. As Katie Lee, Kristy Mullison, Karen Kospo (not real name), and I waited unknowingly in the kitchen, telling naughty jokes as usual, Melanie ran down into the cellar and brought up a gallon of whisky. Katie and I were the only ones to have ever tried alcohol, but we were no veterans of the drinking sport. Melanie, Kristy, and Karen were excited but a little scared about drinking liquor for the first time. We bundled up and plodded down the snowy driveway, carting our contraband across the street to the Sprengle's abandoned Willys Jeep. It took effort to dig out the doors and pry open the frozen hinges. Once inside, the Willys (we pronounced it Willis) provided neither warmth nor comfort—only covering from the fat flakes cascading from the sky. In little time we had no need for warmth anyway. The gallon was drained within twenty minutes. Everything quickly became cozy, fuzzy, and howlingly funny.

Even without alcohol this gang of girls had no problems coming up with things to laugh about. As I will mention elsewhere, because it needs emphasis, we were excellent students, were the stars on winning sports teams, didn't (usually) drink or do drugs, and would be considered "good girls" by most who knew us. But when we got together and out of earshot of adults and our fellow classmates, we had mouths like sailors and reverence for absolutely nothing. This was our way of making up for always following the rules in front of everyone else.

In a condition that magnified all of our impieties, we piled out of the Jeep into a laughing heap in the snow bank, and set forth onto the deserted streets of Steamboat, which by now were concealed in snow. Plows wouldn't come through until just before dawn, and there was already at least five inches on the roads.

From the Sprengle's we weaved our way arm-in-arm through the neighborhood of Crawford Hill (or Snob Knob, as we called it long ago) stopping at homes to bellow our tunes. At least three of us were in choir at school, so we actually presented a decent production with our three-part harmonies. It was the words that got mutilated slightly. *Chestnuts roasting on an open fire* became *Chester's nuts roasting on an open fire*. We changed Rudolf's red body part. And so forth. But we were smart enough to impart the correct words when people opened their doors to listen.

I'd say only 20 percent of the people in their cozy homes would open their doors in ten-degree weather to listen, and we became frustrated that we weren't being given a proper reception.

"Assholes!" I muttered.

"Would you want to stick your ass out here in the cold to listen to our sorry asses?" Karen slurred.

"Yeah!" Kristy roared. "We gotta give them a show. This boring carol shit isn't going to get anybody out here."

"How about we do tricks?" Melanie said with a giggle. "Everyone here but Dori has been a cheerleader."

"Yeah!" we all shouted.

At the next house we formed a human pyramid on the front lawn of a big house. We howled our drunken interpretation of Silent Night until we fell in a laughing heap in the snow. No one even opened the door.

The pyramid thing went unnoticed by four more houses. Our knees and backs were getting tired, but we were sure someone would appreciate our efforts if they would just come outside. Finally at the fifth home, while laughing through some later verse of God Rest Ye Merry Gentlemen with another girl's knee digging into my back, I screamed, "Here comes someone!" A gorgeous, dark man stepped outside with a smile and said in a beautiful foreign accent, "Won't you come inside?"

"Sure!" we cried eagerly, falling in a heap and staggering our way toward the door with snickers, nudges, and whispers such as, "We're all going to get laid!"

Inside was a group of equally good-looking men and women, all in designer sweaters and ski headbands. It turned out they were from Brazil, and were in Steamboat on a long ski vacation. They served us hot rum drinks and asked us questions about American Christmas traditions. They ended up convinced that the caroling pyramid was a common custom. We sat around the fire with silly smiles for an hour's worth of hot liquor and then stumbled out the door yelling Merry Christmas in Portuguese.

Our last stop was the Old Folks Home on Seventh Street. We figured the old farts would be good for a laugh. Besides, they would never turn down anyone, so we would be insured an audience.

We knocked on the front door. The tired countenance of a young nurse lit up when she saw our festive red faces asking if we could carol for the old folks. As we stomped our feet on the entryway carpet, we looked nervously at each other. What if we screwed up, or got the giggles, or fell on our faces? None of us were used to being drunk. We were sure someone would know we were smashed and yell at us for insulting the poor, helpless, old people.

"This is sacrilege," Katie whispered, while the nurse went to line up the wheel chairs.

"Let's make a run for it," I said. "They'll never know what hit them."

"We can't," Karen said. We stood in silence until she added, "We're going to go to hell for this."

We all agreed.

A couple of attendants enthusiastically wheeled a half-dozen sleepy seniors up to us. Before we even started, the old people were pouring thanks on us for coming. They looked as though they hadn't seen another human since last Christmas. And now the first people to give them attention was a group of disrespectful drunk teenagers who had come to get a good laugh at their expense.

Our singing was still choir quality, amazingly enough. From the first song our audience was swaying to the music, clapping their hands, and smiling as if they'd never heard music before. By the second song there were tears in their eyes. There wasn't a hint of mockery on our parts; we sung as if we were trying out for the Mormon Tabernacle Choir. In the end we were asked to give hugs to all the old folks, and some of them wouldn't let go of our hands or stop saying thank you. "This is the best present I'll get this year" one woman told us.

It was late and colder than ever when we walked back outside. The snow had stopped. "Let's go home," Kristy said.

We all agreed and soberly marched back to Melanie's in silence.

Once Christmas was over we still had at least three more months of snow and cold to contend with. We didn't have the luxury of getting sick of outdoor activity or snow sports. Without them cabin fever would conquer us. Legends of folks who'd gone insane or committed suicide during long winters (all winters were long) goaded us to don winter apparel and trudge forth into the white, no matter how sluggish and sun-deprived we felt.

Debi was the family leader in building anything made of snow. Never content with the typical snowman, she once constructed a three-bedroom home under the eaves behind the house. The little kids were able to stand fully erect and pretend to use the little kitchenette inside.

Each year she and Derick would pack a small ski area on the hill behind our house with various size jumps and designated areas for sledding and skiing. I would only participate after the trails were packed and the conditions perfect. But my siblings didn't mind. They were proud to show off their hard work and new tricks on the jumps.

Thanks to her practicing, Debi became at least adept enough at skiing to collect a row of trophies from Steamboat's Winter Carnival, held each year in February. Good old Carl Howelson started up more than a ski hill in Steamboat. In 1914 he began the first annual Winter Carnival, with cross-country skiing and jumping, a tradition that has expanded over the years and continues to this day. Carl was one busy Swede.

I'm not sure what it looked like in Carl's days, but by the time we were old enough to partake in Winter Carnival events (the late 60s and early 70s) the occasion looked like this: traffic on Lincoln Avenue would be shut down, extra snow was hauled in to pack the street for a parade and various skiing events, and the whole town (as far as I knew) came out to watch, bundled in the thickest winter gear they had. The frosty breath of thousands of people spewed forth, and an orchestra of stomping boots (people trying to keep warm) didn't stop until the show was over. For small children there were numerous ski races, and for bigger kids there were assorted events—such as skijouring—in which the skier held a rope that was pulled by a galloping horse. We Duckels kids never arranged to participate in the horse events and so managed to avoid hurtling down the street at 40 mph with snow clods hitting our faces in front of the whole town. But the simple ski races lured us to try for that magnificent trophy the size of a saltshaker depicting a little gold winged lady. I lost every race I tried except for one.

At the start of each race, kids would be lined up right next to each other until an adult with a whistle or flag would signal to go. In an effort to go forward quickly, at least half of the horde would trample on other kids' skis, lose their balance, and end up in pile just after the start. I was always among this pitiful bunch. But in the winter of my tenth year, in cahoots with Debi and with help from Dad, I acquired my one gold trophy in the most challenging of the little kids' events—the three legged race. Debi and I practiced in our driveway for months. Dad helped us tie our legs together with a bandana and cheered us on as we hobbled along. He instructed us in intricate strategies such as bolting ahead at the start to get away from the bunch, having a rhythm to our steps, and in the spirit of basketball, elbowing other contestants who came near us.

"All you gotta do is place third and you'll get a trophy," he reminded us.

On the day of our big race we had plenty of confidence. Dad's coaching worked perfectly. The whistle blew, and we were ahead of the pack in no time, concentrating on our step rhythm and puffing along. I saw nobody ahead of us for most of the race, and was excited and proud and so happy with my sister. But in the end two pairs of boys inched their way ahead of us and beat us. As they were all four on ski teams (and in later years two became Olympians) we didn't feel at all bad about taking home a third place trophy. It looked just like the other ones anyway.

"See? All you had to get was third," Dad said.

After enjoying it in my room for a few years I eventually added the golden lady to Debi's trophy row to help hers look more impressive.

Perhaps my dislike of the cold explains my best winter memory, which involves being very warm—the drive home from Granny and Grampa's on snowy nights. Some winter evenings, maybe twice a week, Dad would take us kids over to our grandparents, perhaps to give Mom a break. He would read the paper, and we would eat candy and be doted upon by Granny and teased by Grampa. ("If you keep eating that candy you're going to get fat like Grampa. If you read too much you'll get big ears like Grampa.")

We'd get ready to leave at bedtime. Dad would head out to his pickup to warm it up, Granny would dress us in our thick outfits, and fifteen minutes later we'd sleepily lumber down the snow-packed path and pile in. Dad kept his truck cab at temperatures exceeding 90 degrees. The hot air lulled us into a half-awake trance by the time we reached the end of Granny's driveway. With four bundled kids nodding off next to him, Dad would absolutely always tune into a basketball game on a scratchy AM station. I would never let myself fall asleep because I couldn't bear to miss the most comforting sounds of that same announcer shouting about basketball with the squeak of tennis shoes in the background and the occasional sounding of the buzzer. Snow was usually dumping from the sky, and in the dark it streamed straight at the windshield like an endless hypnotic tunnel of soft, cool stars. The combination of the hot air, the basketball, the mesmerizing snow, and Dad's constant humming of Christmas tunes even in March was somehow a definition of safety.

Dopers Versus Goat Ropers

Steamboat has long been considered a cow town. Although ranchers no longer drive their herds down the center of Main Street—a practice that continued as late the 1970s—there are still cattle ranches surrounding the area, men and women who wear cowboy hats and boots everyday whether there is a rodeo happening or not, a pro-rodeo most weekends in the summer, and pickups in every other parking space. The People Who Promote Tourism try zealously to keep Steamboat's "Cowboy Place" image intact by slathering horses, barbed wire fences, and cowboy hats all over every slick brochure concerning the place. These brochures sell expensive cowboyish clothes, real estate, furniture, meals, and recreation that no real cowboy could ever afford. But although the rich and uninventive have claimed the cowboy image (and Steamboat) as their own, many of the original families of Routt County live much as they always have—

enjoying the beautiful country and letting the tourists and newcomers think what they want.

The Duckels were never real ranchers or cowboys but we seemed to fit in with them. We were too square to fit in with the city-slickers who moved to Steamboat to ski and start an outdoorsy lifestyle. My first friend was Kim Wilhelm, the cowgirl who froze on the Christmas tree hunt with me. I began playing with her at the age of three. A tiny blond-haired girl with big brown eyes, she was a year older than I, and a foot shorter. I constantly felt ugly around Kim because anyone who saw us would say about her, "Oh she's the cutest little girl I've ever seen" and nothing about me. Her cowboy parents, Patsy and Willie, grew up with my father in Steamboat and married before they were out of high school. Willie worked in the coalmines west of Steamboat and ranched the whole time I knew him, and Patsy drove the Elk River school bus, built camps for hunters, ran sleigh rides, ranched and took care of four kids.

When we weren't running from her three wild older brothers, Kim and I were playing in her Gramma Truax's big red barn, and from its hayloft we would jump into scratchy, pokey piles of hay. We'd sneak cream off the top of the newly bottled milk that waited in Gramma's mudroom to be sold to neighbors. As little girls we'd gather eggs from the chicken coop, milk the cows—which I could never do properly—make forts in the hayloft, ride horses, and occasionally try our hand at jumping cow pies the size of a small automobile. Sometimes we'd play on the farm equipment or taunt the geese. Cowboys were generally not skiers, so in the winter we'd snowmobile. When I was young I didn't see any of our pastimes as country or cowboy. It was just fun.

There was only one radio station available in Steamboat back then—KRAI out of Craig, Colorado—over 40 miles away—and they played one kind of music. Country. Old country. With a background of scratchy AM noise we heard The Sons of the Pioneers, Hank Williams, Johnny Horton, Patsy Cline, and the rest of them. At that time these songs were not revered or looked on as classic, soulful relics—they were just music.

"God damn it!" Mom would yell. "I get so sick of these whining rednecks. When are they going to get another radio station?"

"What's wrong with it, Mommy?" I'd ask.

"It's shitty," she'd answer, and I'd leave it at that.

Eventually Mom found a solution to the country music monopoly. She acquired some Simon and Garfunkle albums, along with the New Christy Minstrels, Judy Collins, and Carole King, which she listened to so much they turned whitish and skipped every other line. I still sing some of the songs with the same few words missing.

By the time I was in Junior High (that would be the 1970s) all kinds of music seeped up to the mountains. And all kinds of people. Long-haired ski bums and progressive families came to Steamboat to get out of the rat race, and if you asked my Dad, they were all hippies. We learned to refer to any male without a crew cut, and any woman who skied better than she cooked, as a hippie. Cowboys were the people who'd lived in Steamboat forever, or who lived on ranches, or who wore cowboy hats, or hung around with cowboys, or hated hippies. Any one of the criteria was enough for general classification. Although my family met only a few of the requirements, we definitely ran with the cowboys. I think Mom fancied herself a part-time hippie, and for a while actually collected a few hippie friends, but being married to Fred Duckels left her no way to fully experience pure hippie-ness. A Steamboat native with a crew cut even in the late 60s,

Dad made daily derogatory remarks about hippies. The Steamboat Pilot once wrote, "Fred Duckels claims he can jump 50 hippies with a D9." A D9 is a bulldozer. The heaviest, biggest one made at the time.

"Why can't you grow your hair, Dad?" we'd ask him.

"Because I don't want to look like a hippie."

"But it's cool. It's groovy."

"I don't do things because everyone else does."

"Uncle Chuck has long hair. And a mustache. Why don't you grow a mustache?"

"I'm not a sheep."

The cowboy/hippie rivalry was well summed up in an inscription scraped into the paint of a stall in the girl's bathroom of our junior high.

I'd rather be a doper than a goat roper.

The half-court line of our gymnasium divided our junior high dances straight down the middle—one side for cowboys doing the country swing, and the other for hippies doing everything else. The DJ switched every other song to please both audiences; one country song, one hippie song. I would go to the dances, but no boys ever asked me to dance, so I didn't have to choose a side. Did I mention Junior High sucked?

In Junior High I lived a double life. At school I turned against my hick heritage and told people I hated country music. Listening to Chicago, Three Dog Night, Bachman Turner Overture, and the Carpenters was deemed a serious survival skill: it helped lessen the regular adolescent ridicule I received, if only by a fraction. In those days when the slightest infraction of un-coolness could make or break your entire life, I did my best to come across as hip.

141

But away from those halls of convention I would secretly swoon over Tanya Tucker, Merle Haggard, and Charlie Pride. My cowboy friends, Kim Wilhelm and Jolene Stetson, never wavered from their devotion to their heritage, even in front of the vicious pubescents at school. But I suspect they weren't nearly as insecure as I was.

Also during my junior high years, on Friday evenings in the summer, I would ride Casey, our ancient horse, the two miles from our house at Fish Creek into town. I'd pay one dollar to be a competitor in a gymkhana, or mini-rodeo. I am still baffled at the thought of myself as an unconfident, gangly teenager gathering the self-assurance to participate (regularly) in events I was sure to lose, and in front of a real—although small—crowd. I went by myself, and not once did a friend or family member ever come to watch me. When I remind my family today that I actually did partake in this sport, everyone but Mom shake their heads in disbelief. "I sure don't remember that," they say. I must not have bragged about it much. Mom encouraged me to keep at it; I think she was proud of me.

The gymkhanas were held at the rodeo grounds near Howelson Hill. I entered every event I could, including barrel racing and other timed events. Anything that didn't involve roping a calf was available to me. I placed dead last in every single event I competed in, every gymkhana. There is a good chance that several women out there, near to me in age, are to this day laughing about the summers when Dori Duckels brought her near-dead horse out to compete.

In barrel racing, the object is to get around three barrels—spaced around the ring in a triangle—in the shortest amount of time. Whatever the second to the last girl's time was, I would generally double it. At the time it didn't occur to me that this was even slightly funny. I assumed people should know that my horse was old and that, of course, I did not take these events too seriously. But I imagine every real competitor, the fans, and especially the announcers up in the box had to work hard to keep their laughter from spilling out. They must have been stupefied at my audacity (and my cruelty for dragging that poor old horse out there). Not one of the cowgirls, whom I knew peripherally at school, would ever speak a word to me. They must have been mortified at my weird behavior. Jolene Stetson, a good friend, would always be too busy getting her horse ready or helping her mother, father, brothers and sister with their events and livestock to spend much time with me. I don't ever remember being lonely, though. I kind of liked watching from the sidelines and being somehow anonymous. Away from the noise of home and pressure to be cool at school, it was one place I knew no one would bother me.

Now that I think about it, Casey would have probably preferred the glue factory to the Friday Torture Arena. That old guy had to walk two miles into town, spend hours standing around in a saddle and every once in a while be forced to sprint around (more of a lope, really) while my bony legs flailed up and down on his sides. He was stubborn when it came to any sort of exercise, and I had to kick like a wrecking ball on both of his sides to get him to trot. He made sure I never got near that $15 prize. When it was all over, I'd say goodbye to all my friends (that would be nobody) and we'd ride the two very steep miles back home. He might have hated me.

Usually we'd get home after dark. When we'd reach our driveway he'd break into a dash faster than I could ever have made him run at the rodeo, because he knew his special rodeo treat—oats—was waiting for him. While he munched

I'd unsaddle and comb him and then take him down to his corral and throw him a third bale of hay. I'd spank his butt. I'd walk up the trail back to the house and turn around one more time to see his dark swayback silhouette and his head hanging low.

Then I'd go inside and join the noise.

Mom's Hippie Friends were a temporary distraction from her life as a housewife, mother of four, spouse of a proud hayseed, and inhabitant of a small, rural town. They came into her life in 1971, when I was eight. Mom was 28. Dawn and Gretchen were maids at the Anchor Motel, a little place by the Yampa River, which was owned by Mom's friend Arlene. The four women would sit around the kitchen table in the owner's apartment and talk. I remember that they bad-mouthed hicks, organized religion, small town mentalities, the trod-upon housewife mindset, and institutions of most kinds. By their mannerisms and laughter I knew it was exciting, funny, naughty, and rebellious, and that my mom was loving every minute of it. I think she felt like she finally found people who understood her—at least for a little while.

To give Mom a little time off, the two hippie women offered to take Debi and me for a couple nights in the woods. They claimed they wanted to experience children, who were the only ones with true innocence.

Dawn was a tall, beautiful, thin woman with long, flowing black hair. Gretchen, a sandy-colored woman with braids, was a foot shorter and not as pretty as Dawn. Gretchen followed Dawn around like a puppy. So did I. I thought Dawn was a living Barbie Doll (she probably would have killed me if I had told her so) and I wanted to look like her when I grew up. The fact that she wore no make-up and her clothes were found in a dumpster made no difference. Her grace showed through. So I was thrilled to be invited for a weekend with my idol.

"We'll pick the girls up at 5:00," Dawn reminded my mom one day at the Anchor Motel.

"See you then," my mom said, trying to conceal her joy at having two fewer children making noise for a while.

Dawn and Gretchen showed up at 8:30. Mom didn't care that they were late. Her free-living friends did what they wanted to, when they wanted to, and that was as it should be.

"Where are you going camping?" Mom asked as Debi and I filed out the door with our backpacks.

"Hot Springs," they replied.

"How are you getting there without a car?"

"Hitchhiking."

"Great! Have fun!" Mom said, and closed the door. (Remember, hitchhiking really was a safe and common means of transportation in Steamboat back then.)

As we walked away from the door in the near-darkness I said, "Where's your car?"

"We don't have one," Living Barbie said.

"Why not?"

"We don't need one. We walk or we get a ride."

"Where's your camping stuff?" I asked.

"We don't need things."

I didn't ask any more.

Little Debi, 7 at the time, said, "Do we have to walk all the way to the Hot Springs?"

"Nah. We'll get a ride."

We set out into the crisp summer night, our light jackets and brisk pace keeping us reasonably warm. Dawn and Gretchen began a conversation about astrology, and Debi and I, with nothing to contribute, just listened. We stared up at the stars on the crystal clear night and would point occasionally at especially bright ones, or at the beautiful Milky Way.

On and on they blabbered—oblivious to our youthful innocence —about houses and risings and ascendants, and moons, and suns and planets. They had seemed so sincere about wanting to take us for the weekend. I didn't understand why they lost interest in us the minute we set out.

I remembered one Astrology thing they were talking about, because it kind of scared me.

"And what is the eighth house again?" Gretchen asked.

"Don't you remember? It's Death." Dawn said.

By the time we rounded the corner where Strawberry Park began and the neighborhoods of Steamboat ended, it was pitch black. At that time the road wasn't paved and Strawberry Park was nothing but nature, with no lights anywhere in sight.

"Are you sure someone will come along?" I uttered the first words in a half hour.

"Sure. Now will you two be quiet and quit worrying?"

After ten more minutes of trying to follow Dawn's crappy flashlight, an old beat-up 1940s pick-up truck stopped for us. A grizzly old hippy offered us a ride. Dawn and Gretchen sat in the cab. Debi and I sat in the bed with the dogs.

Steamboat gets chilly at night, even in the summertime. We had already been chattering our teeth a little, but after we piled in the filthy pick-up and sped off, we were cold. Debi and I bundled together and hoped the ride would end soon. The driver pushed his ancient vehicle to its limits on the windy dirt road, and we fishtailed on the curves and bounced around on the washboard hills. The dogs, two Labradors, continually careened into our little bodies as they were thrown from one side of the bed to the other. Dawn and Gretchen never looked back at us.

Finally the truck pulled over to the side of the road, let us out, and took off in a cloud of dust.

"Is this where we wanted to go?" I asked. Debi was afraid to open her mouth.

"Yeah. We're going up there," Dawn said, pointing to a skinny trail that led into the black woods.

"Doesn't that go to the old cabins?" I asked.

"Sure does," they said.

"Those are abandoned. Did you buy them?"

"No."

I didn't ask any more questions.

We stumbled through the aspen and fern forest with our ever-dimming flashlight. It was way past our bedtime and Debi and I felt like we were sleeping while standing up. Eventually we spotted a fire through the trees, and Debi and I pinched each other with happiness. By the time we reached the campfire we saw that the old cabins were being used as homes for Dawn, Gretchen, and a whole bunch of other hippies with equally long hair and yucky clothes.

"How are you little girls doing?" one of the men said.

"They've been complaining a lot," Dawn said.

"Can we go to bed?" I asked.

"We're tired," Debi added.

"Follow me." Gretchen led us into one of the cabins where we were instructed to sleep together on the bottom bunk of a twin bunk-bed. We crawled in and went to sleep instantly.

The next morning we awoke early and waited out by the dead campfire for hours before anyone got up.

"What's for breakfast?" Debi asked.

"I'll cook it for you," Dawn said. My hopes for a plate of scrambled eggs and bacon were dashed when, 45 minutes later, Dawn handed us a pan of crunchy brown rice with nothing on it.

"This is breakfast?" I asked.

"Don't complain," Dawn said. "We don't have money so we get our food out of the Safeway dumpster. We take what we find."

"Couldn't you find any bacon?" Debi asked.

"We don't eat bacon."

"Why? Bacon's the best food in the world."

Dawn smirked and looked at her hippie companions. "They want to know why we don't eat meat."

"We just don't," Gretchen said.

We stopped asking questions and choked down the rice.

That day we watched several hippies make colorful candles over the fire. (We were not allowed to help but we could watch). After lunch of crunchy brown rice, we were bored and went into the cabin to play by ourselves. Dawn and Gretchen were on the top bunk studying astrology. We crawled into our bottom bunk and after 15 minutes of whispering and giggling about yucky brown rice and lumpy candles, we started listening in on the conversation of the granola girls up top.

"God is everywhere and in everything," we heard Gretchen say.

"Absolutely," Dawn said.

Boredom prompted me to chime in. "Oh yeah? Is he in this pillow?"

Silence from the top bunk.

"Hi! I'm God!" Debi said in a high voice, walking her pillow toward me.

"No, I'm God!" I said in a low voice, making my pillow look more menacing than hers.

"Me! I'm God!"

"No, me!"

"Oh yeah? Well take this!" Debi bonked me on the head with her pillow.

"Hey! You're not supposed to hit God!" I flung my pillow across her face.

"Cut it out down there!" Dawn said. "You are so immature."

"What does that mean?" Debi asked.

"Just shut up." Gretchen said.

For a few minutes we whispered and giggled about the God in our pillows. Then we began listening in again.

"And what's the eighth house again?" Gretchen asked.

We heard no answer.

"Death," I called out.

We heard nothing from them again, so we went outside to break sticks in the woods.

After a dinner of crunchy brown rice (which was beginning to taste a little moldy) we went to bed, looking forward to going home the next day. The next morning the crunchy brown rice was hard to force down, and we ate very little, knowing that a real meal would be coming by lunchtime. After breakfast we were informed that we were going swimming at the Hot Springs.

As we set out down the trail through the trees Debi noticed that the women had no swimming gear with them.

"Where are your swimming suits?" she asked.

The girls smirked. "We aren't going to wear them," Dawn said.

"You're going to go naked?" I asked.

"We not ashamed of our bodies. The human body is a beautiful thing."

This was a new concept to me. Debi and I looked at each other and shrugged our shoulders. I was secretly a little scared.

At that time the Hot Springs was a primitive series of stone pools, their heat regulated by the varying mixture of hot water from a spring that runs out of the side of the mountain and cool water from a stream that flows to meet it. The Hot Springs was known to be the Naked Hippy Hang-Out in those times. It was free and open to everyone. (Today it is an expensive, fancy resort thingy.)

When we arrived at the spring, Debi and I hid behind a bush to get into our suits, while the hippy chicks tossed off their smelly clothes and stepped right in the water. We took one look at the ladies' black pubic hair and burst out giggling. After our suits were adjusted and sure not to expose any embarrassing body parts, we tiptoed over the grass and rocks saying "ouch ouch ouch" until we plunged into the very warm water. Dawn and Gretchen spent most of our meditative, relaxation dip complaining about how disgusting it was that children had to be ashamed of nudity. They explained over and over how wonderful the human body was, emphasizing the closeness to nature one feels when one is naked, and the joy of being unashamed. We got so sick of the lecture that we tipped our heads back just enough so that our ears were under water and we couldn't hear them. Debi and I eyed each other and pretended to be fascinated with what they were saying while kicking each other under water.

Soon another bather arrived. A 50-year-old man. When he began to undress, Debi and I got very interested in blowing bubbles under water and looking into the woods in the opposite direction. Once he got in the water, he swam by himself for while in a pool about 20 feet away, so we missed having to see his unclothed body for a while. Instead we got Round 2 of the nudity lecture, which this time included examples of famous art we'd never seen, and the mention of the animal kingdom. Soon Mr. Naked decided to sun himself on a big rock near us. Dawn and Gretchen took this opportunity to glorify his lack of inhibition and strongly suggested we look over at him to experience how good he must feel to have the sun nourishing his entire body.

Debi looked first. I saw a look of surprise on her face, thinly disguised with nonchalance. Dawn and Gretchen took the opportunity to make fun of me and praise Debi for her open-mindedness. I reluctantly turned my head slowly over in the man's direction. There I saw a gray-haired man with long gray pubic hairs and a big boner. He was waving and smiling at the four of us. At the time I was too young to understand that it wasn't just the sun nourishing his body.

This was the first naked man I'd ever seen. I tried to put on Debi's pretend air of detachment, but I was quite shocked. I stared for some time, trying to file the strange image in a place in my mind where it might be comfortable, but it took some convincing of my little brain that it was even real. A real naked man! And smiling!

Once I accepted the reality of the situation, Debi and I went about our business, swimming underwater and blowing bubbles to avoid Dawn and Gretchen. We had grown to hate them. To our delight, we soon were told to get dressed; they were going to take us home.

We walked down the skinny dirt road in the shade of the aspens. I commented about how the wind in the aspens sounded like bacon cooking. Dawn told me not to mention bacon again. It took no time to catch a ride in a cramped, open-air Jeep with a couple of young guys. While Debi and I sat cramped in the small space behind the back seat, anxious to get home, bonking our knees on beer cans and each other, the girls and guys laughed and made plans.

"We're going to make a stop on the way home," Dawn told us.

"Where are we going?" Debi asked

"You'll see."

Once we got into town the Jeep pulled into the driveway of one of the many small, non-descript houses near the hospital.

"Why aren't you taking us home?" I said. "Our house is only a few blocks from here."

"Quit being so impatient. We've got important stuff to do," Dawn said, and then they all laughed.

Walking up to the house, Debi and I purposely squished weeds that grew up through the sidewalk. A ripped screen door banged shut behind us as we walked into a living room with stained carpet, no furniture, and 15 hippies sitting in a circle on the floor.

"Hey man, what's with the little people?" said a slow-speaking, bearded, skinny guy with no shirt.

"We'll get rid of them pretty soon," Gretchen said as she and Dawn hugged some of the guys.

Debi and I found a place in the circle and gave each other the bored look. An hour went by. The grown-ups talked on and on and laughed more than they should have. I tapped my foot, and Debi picked at the thread hanging from her shirt. We sighed a few times. I looked outside at the lovely sunshine and wished we were in our backyard playing in the sprinkler.

"Wanna puff?" a male voice said in my ear.

I looked to my left to see a droopy-eyed guy smiling at me. He presented me with a withered-looking cigarette on a metal stick. I didn't understand. He was a grown-up. Surely he knew I didn't smoke cigarettes. I looked at Debi. She had a look of terror on her face. The guy next to her reached over and grabbed the cigarette.

"Don't listen to him, girlies. He's from a different planet," he said as he began sucking smoke.

Debi and I went back to being bored, and eventually hungry. I rounded my back and rolled back and forth a few times but the carpet was wet behind me so I stopped. I flapped the back of my shirt for a while to try to dry it. Debi rested her chin on a hand and nodded off a few times. After the cigarette had passed by us three more times, we whispered to each other for a second. I pinched Debi's leg. She winced. She rose like an old woman and walked with her head down over to Dawn. She leaned down and said something in Dawn's ear.

"Oh God. Will somebody please take these little whiners back to their house?"

"Where do they live?" a man's voice said.

"Somewhere on Spruce Street, I think."

"I'll give them a ride," said the guy from another planet. "Somebody got a car?"

A set of keys flew from across the room and hit him on the head. Everyone laughed and laughed and laughed. It wasn't *that* funny. We said good-bye to our camping buddies as we walked out the door, but they didn't respond. Gretchen was making out with one of the Jeep guys, and Dawn just stared right through us.

Besides the Jeep, there were four ugly old cars outside the house. We got situated in one but the key wouldn't go into the ignition. The man thought it was hilarious, and we had to wait for him to stop laughing before getting out and trying another car. And another. The third car, a VW Beetle, started and we weaved our way home. We told him where to turn and which house was ours.

"Who was that?" Mom said as we came in the front door.

"Some man. He lives over by the hospital," I said.

"Was he camping with you?"

"No."

"Why did he give you a ride?"

"Dawn and Gretchen told him to."

"Where are Dawn an Gretchen?"

"At his house."

"What were you doing there? I thought you were supposed to be camping."

"They wanted to stop there on the way home to smoke cigarettes."

"Oh."

"They were weird. They all smoked the same cigarette."

"What?"

"They sat in a circle and passed the same cigarette around. Is it because they're poor?"

Mom stared for a moment. She had an angry look on her face.

"Mom?"

"What!"

"Is it because they're poor? Do they get their cigarettes out of a dumpster, too?"

"No, they don't get their cigarettes out of a goddamned dumpster. They can't afford food or clothes or a car, but they can afford...expensive goddamned cigarettes."

"How do you know they're expensive?" Debi asked, but Mom was headed for the phone in the dining room to call Arlene at the Anchor Motel. Mom stretched the long phone cord into the kitchen. We followed, curious.

"Arlene. Guess what those free and easy bitches did?" She saw us. "Get outside you two! Now!" We ran out into the back yard and stood under the open kitchen window. We heard snippets such as "goddamn" and "shitty" and "little kids for Christ's sake." All we understood was that there would be no more camping trips with Dawn and Gretchen.

We rolled around the in the grass yelling, "Weeeeeee!"

Tricks and Lies

Fred Duckels loves to play tricks on people. He handed down this appreciation to his children, but had no idea of the lengths to which we would carry on his legacy. He never knew about most of the stunts we did; had he known he would have been proud. Thinking up funny things, crazy things, and often mean things in order to surprise people was a science and an art for us, and we tried hard to perfect it.

Apparently Dad has always loved practical jokes, and from our Granny we heard stories of his greatest hits. The best one was, not surprisingly, pretty mean. He was a very quiet boy, difficult to coax into speaking a word. A little girl came to visit and according to Granny, had her eye on young Freddie. After a long visit of mostly silence Fred approached the little girl when the adults were in another room. He handed her a pair of binoculars and asked if she'd like to look through them. She was shocked and delighted that Fred had opened up to her and gladly took the binoculars and looked through them out the big picture window. When she put them down she gazed at Fred with two black ink rings around her eyes and didn't know it until her parents saw her. I guess it took a long time for the ink to wear off. I think Dad got in trouble, but I'm sure he thought it was worth it.

Our training began young. When we were small children he was fond of giving us "whisker kisses," a painful and smelly pastime. This supposedly affectionate undertaking involved snatching us up by our arm as we innocently walked by his rocking chair, scooping us in his arms, and kissing us. To the untrained eye it might have looked harmless, but this sport took place only when he had returned from a long day of working construction. His beard would be the texture of 60-grit sandpaper, and he would smell like he'd been drinking diesel fuel and eating bologna sandwiches all day. He made sure to rub his whiskers all over our young, tender faces for at least five minutes, and he would emit a noisy, high-pitched, evil laugh while saying, "You win first place! You get a whisker kiss!" When deposited back on the floor we would hold our crimson faces in our hands and yell at him. He would laugh higher and louder about how lucky we were to have won first place. I usually went to the bathroom to wash the stink off my face and took time to feel cold water on my whisker burn.

Most of the time we stayed far, far from Dad's rocking chair. Once in a while an unlucky child would forget what lurked within a four-foot radius of that spot. If Dad noticed a naïve victim absent-mindedly wandering within the reaches of his clutch, he would hold his newspaper higher and stiller, like a cat ready to pounce. Abruptly he'd throw the paper down and make his move. We rarely got away. I remember as I got older how I fought harder to squirm away, and I am to this day amazingly talented at wrenching my wrist from the grasp of someone's hand. I am almost convinced that I got away once, but it could be a wishful dream I made up.

If sufficient time elapsed without a whisker kiss, Dad would begin hunting for prey.

"Dori, guess what?"

"What?"

"You win first place"

I'd run.

"Don't you want your prize? I might have to give first place to someone else." he would yell across the house.

All the kids would run.

Truthfully, even though it was gross, we didn't mind it that much. It was a sport, after all, and mostly we liked to see Dad laugh. He's retirement age now, and all of us are old enough to grow 60-grit stubble somewhere on our bodies, and he still tells us we've won first place once in a while. We usually say, "That's disgusting," and he laughs high and loud and evil.

Instead of using the Boogie Man to scare us, Dad invented the Snow Snake. He never told us what it looked like or what it could actually do to us—only that it could get us. I pictured a giant white serpent as big around as a car tire and as long as a house. I figured it would swallow me. Dad would yell, "Watch out for Snow Snakes!" when we left the house, or when he came home from work, he'd ask if we'd seen any that day. Only when we were very young did we believe this myth. He couldn't hide his wicked grin when he spoke of it, and this was a tell-tale sign he was up to something. I think the Snow Snake was the only one of Dad's jokes that Mom thought was funny.

"Hey! I brought home something to show you," he said as he walked in the front door from his usual long day at work. "This'll teach you about electricity." Then he walked right back out the door.

"Oh, shit," Mom said.

All four of us, ranging in ages from three to ten, ran out into the driveway to see what he was up to. He placed on the gravel and started setting up an electric device of some sort, similar to a car battery.

"You better not hurt them!" Mom shouted from the kitchen window.

"See, this here's a blah-be-tee-blah and what happens is..." He went on about circuits and currents and conductors, and we pretended to listen. "Now one of you hold this metal thing here. It's connected to the blah-be-tee-blah."

I eagerly grabbed it.

"Now Dori, you stand on my right. Who wants to hold the other one?"

Derick took it.

"Now Dana and Debi, you stand in between them and hold hands with them."

We stood like innocent ducks in a shooting gallery while he giggled.

"Now we're only going to try this on low power at first. You tell me if you feel anything."

"Damnit Fred! Cut it out!" Mom said.

We were all smiling, thinking that hands-on experiments were neato.

He flipped a switch, and I felt a tingling throughout my body. Dad started giggling again. "See? You all felt it, didn't you? That's because..." and he went on about circuits and currents and conductors, and we interrupted him and told him to turn up the power.

"OK, just a little bit. Why don't you trade places?"

We rearranged ourselves so Derick and I were in the middle.

Dad turned up the juice, and his laugh got higher and louder. He flipped the switch again. This time I felt my body hair rising and my teeth felt prickly. Dad shut off the power.

"That's it." Mom came out of the house. "Put that thing away now. You're going to cook them."

"But Mom, it's fun," I said. "It doesn't hurt. It really doesn't."

I think Dad agreed with her because he started packing it up, all the while giggling. He giggled as he put the gadget away in his truck. We all begged him to try it again and turn up the power.

"No, I think you understand electricity now."

"Yeah, great lesson," Mom said.

He spent the rest of the evening asking each of us what it felt like. He couldn't stop giggling about our answers. Now that Mom knew that the danger of seeing her children turned into pieces of charcoal had passed, she perked up an ear to hear us.

"My mind felt funny, and it made me happy," three-year-old Dana said.

"I liked it," I said. "I want to go around like that all day."

On a normal evening the entire family went in different directions—Dad read the paper, Derick played imaginary football in the basement, I painted my nails for the forth time that day, Dana played with Fisher-Price toys, Mom read Advanced Astrology and Metaphysical Musings for Lovers of the Occult, and Debi disappeared into thin air. But on this night we all lounged in the living room near Dad where we could rejoice in the sound of his laughter and keep it going all night by embellishing and exaggerating our tales of being electrocuted. I think we all went to bed happy.

Thinking up mischievous pranks was an important bonding pastime for Debi and me. We fought quite a bit, but an easy truce was available when we had a hankering to imagine a new creative way to play a joke on someone. We tried countless times to dip the fingers of our sleeping siblings into a glass of warm water (in an effort to get them to pee the bed) but the desired results were never realized. Melanie Sprengle swore it had worked on her brother Jimmy Joe, but we weren't sure we believed her after we tried it 19 times. Sneaking up on Derick and Dana while they were playing and then throwing toys or sticks at them was fun. A few times we watched them get in a fight because Dana would be convinced that Derick had done the throwing. But usually we got caught.

The getting caught was always anti-climactic. The most thrilling moments in the process was thinking up the idea and beginning to implement the plan. We would practically choke with sneaky laughter and delight in the intricate ins and outs of our proposal. (We usually came up with an elaborate, convoluted, well-timed design that basically amounted to something like "sneak up on Derick and Dana and throw stuff at them.") Our hearts would race as we'd creep in for the kill. Holding in our laughter was terribly difficult as we peeked at each other knowingly from our designated hiding places. Most times we'd throw and miss. Derick and Dana would notice nothing, which was of course cause for an outrageous adrenaline rush, as if we'd aimed at a killer lion on an African safari and lost another bullet. Once we finally hit our target, our victims would say, with no emotion whatsoever, "What was that?" In the planning of our schemes we always imagined our victim's response to be a melodramatic display of consternation. They were supposed to be baffled, ruffled, and in awe of the great mystery that was befalling them. They would act just like those hilarious people on Candid Camera. This *never* happened for us, but we never gave up trying. Invariably, unless we caused them to get in a fight (which was a huge success, in our eyes) Derick and Dana would calmly and uneventfully declare that Dori and Debi were up to something and go back to their playing. Sometimes we'd jump out to surprise them, but they'd ignore us or tell us to cut it out. Not quite what we'd envisioned.

Small, mostly unsuccessful tricks on the little kids included running a bunch of string across their bedroom door so they couldn't get out, slipping a tape-recorder under their bed and playing the "chilling thrilling sounds of the haunted house," putting food under their bed to rot, and moving all the items around in their room. The results: They broke the string immediately and had fun doing it, were excited that we left the tape-recorder because they could make their own tape, never noticed the rotten food because they had enough of their own putrid food under the bed to drown out the smell, and took no notice at all of the moved objects. Debi and I had to face the fact that our greatest glee in our schemes would be attained in the idea stage. It did not slow us down.

Our biggest failure at our jokes was so colossal in its downfall that it took years to overcome the shame and degradation of the outcome. It took place at the New House, when Debi and I were in junior high. Our basement bedrooms finally had drywall over the studs; Debi and I had our own rooms, and Derick and Dana shared one. For the fiftieth time we thought we'd try the old short-sheet-the-bed trick on Derick. It had never worked. He didn't care if he used a sheet. So we thought we'd add a creative touch to the joke and sprinkle a little sand in his bed. We thought that surely he'd not miss this funny part of the trick, and along with the short sheet we'd all have a grand chuckle. Well, he noticed. And he was mad. He screamed at us and ran upstairs and told Dad. We were sure that Dad, being the prankster that he was, would find the whole farce quite amusing and tell Derick to get over it. Dad was real real mad. We were mystified at how seriously he took the situation. He took it so seriously that he actually told us he was going to think of a terrible punishment for us. We were mortified and offered to do what we'd planned on doing all along: to clean it up. He decided that yes, we'd clean it up, along with the dirty shambles of a room in the basement we called The Dungeon in order to make a nice new room for our dear, trod-upon brother, Derick.

The Dungeon was dark. It had no windows, and the little humidity that Colorado had all seemed to congregate there and fester. It was stacked to the ceiling with boxes of junk, discarded toys, and general rubble of all kinds. When we'd moved from the Old House, all the broad-spectrum crap that couldn't be placed elsewhere ended up there. We were instructed to make it a very nice, livable room. We worked and worked and worked for weeks. We found disgusting, indecipherable items that we picked up with rubber gloves, pinched noses, and wide-open garbage sacks. We wrapped bandanas around our faces while sweeping up billowing clouds of stinky dust. We hauled stacks and boxes and heaps and piles of old ridiculous, meaningless debris. We came to know the meaning of the word pack-rat and vowed never to partake in the hobby. It took all of our free time for quite a while, and although we begged Dad to let us off the hook he never wavered.

In the end the room was so adorable we wanted it to be ours. We laid a relatively livable rug down and had a nice bedside table with a vase of flowers on it. It didn't sparkle, but was a remarkable transformation. I think Dad might have been impressed, but didn't dare let on. The job was our punishment, and the reward we received was to be off the hook. Once Derick moved in and started depositing his usual accouterments such as rotten food under the bed, piles of stinky clothes, and stacks of discarded toys, the room regained some of its original character. The name of the room remains The Dungeon, and will remain for all eternity.

Our most successful trick has been remembered and recited over and over and with relish, mostly because our successes were so infrequent. Our pride and joy was the day we climbed up on the roof of the New House and pelted six-year-old Dana with bologna slices, raw eggs, small tomatoes, and grapes. Due to some magical alignment of the planets our aim was true on every toss. A soaring egg would hit her shoulder and explode, sending yellow and goo all over her hair and face. The bologna stuck to her head or back, and colorful fruit stains lit up her t-shirt. She ran back and forth along the side of the house, not knowing from whence the barrage was coming, thus keeping her in prime target range. Even though shaken by hysterical laughter we still could not miss. We were glad we'd hauled a couple dozen eggs and whole pack of bologna so we wouldn't run out of ammunition. If Dana had showed signs of misery we'd have let up, but she seemed to be enjoying it. She giggled as she was pummeled and looked everywhere except up for the source. She seemed to think of it as a game. This may have been the only time when one of our plots didn't backfire or fizzle. Strangely Mom didn't detect that the refrigerator was half empty, Dana didn't tattle, and we got all the clothes in the washer before anyone was the wiser. All of our conspiring over all those years was made worth it in this one single episode, never to be equaled again. Which is not to say we didn't keep trying.

I've kept a secret until now. There was a cabin across the road and up the hill from our house, maybe a third of a mile away. We knew that people came and went from it very infrequently; we surmised that some city-slicker owned it and came for a stay two or three times a year. Its log construction and isolation made it the quintessential Colorado mountain cabin. From the rocking chairs on the front porch one peeked through the surrounding aspens to see a sweeping vista of the Yampa Valley. It was well-kept considering that it was vacant most of the time.

Mercedes Thompson and I daringly decided to investigate the premises one summer day, quite sure that our luck wouldn't betray us with a visit from the owner. We had heard a rumor that the owners were going to sell the cabin anyway. We knocked at the front door and yelled "hello hello hello" to make sure it was empty. The door was not locked. We peeked our heads in and silently walked into the living room. Furnished with regular stuff—sofa, lazy-boy, rug, table, some blankets—the place looked orderly and lived in. Partly burned logs sat in a beautiful stone fireplace. It couldn't have been that long since someone had been there. We walked into the small kitchen to find the cupboards filled with food, but the refrigerator was empty. A stale smell hung about, but nothing unusual for a log cabin with a fireplace.

After deciding that no one was here or going to come, we decided to do a little baking. We pulled out of the cupboards flour, water, red chili peppers, evaporated milk, Vienna sausage, powdered sugar, and crunched up bay leaves and mixed them in a bowl. We were just looking for a way to start up the gas stove when we heard a car coming up the drive. Mercedes and I stood paralyzed and staring at each other as we listened to a car door slam and footsteps coming toward the house. I remember no time when I panicked so completely. Mercedes and I clutched each other and whimpered like cowardly cartoon characters. We scrambled in circles for a few seconds and then raced for the bathroom and into the shower. We both began crying, certain that we would be thrown in jail. We hugged each other for comfort and tried to still our shaking. Then we heard a knock at the door.

"It must be a stranger or they wouldn't knock!" I whispered.

"We gotta act cool," Mercedes said as we climbed out of the shower. "Act like we own the place. You look older than me. You do the talking." I was fourteen, but I was nearly 5'10" and had been known to pass for 24 when I wanted to. I didn't argue, but would have loved an excuse to back down.

I opened the door with what I imagined to be a calm expression. There stood a thin man with a beard—a typical Colorado 70's guy.

"What are you doing here?" he said.

"We live here," I said as if it was obvious.

"But I was going to buy this house. I've been looking at it for a while."

"Well, sorry. I guess we got here first." I didn't want to add much. I was terrified and wanted him to leave as soon as possible. He was kind of trying to peek around me.

"Wow. You bought my house."

"Yep. Sorry."

He looked bewildered and pensive. "Well, OK. Thanks anyway."

"Sure. No problem."

I closed the door as he walked off the porch and looked at Mercedes with bulging eyes, my heart hammering in my chest, cussing ten obscene words in a row. We peeked through the curtains as we saw his car pull away, and when we were sure that he was gone we tore out the door like Goldilocks. We had not one thought about the baking mess we'd made. We ran as fast as we could back to my house, saying mostly, "Oh my God!" and "Oh my Gosh!" We began walking nonchalantly as we reached our driveway. We went straight to my bedroom where we whispered for the rest of the day, replaying the incident over and over, still in shock.

It took months before I rested easier about the episode. Anyone's mention of the cabin or even the road to it was like police sirens to a criminal. I'd go rigid and my ears would be like the Bionic Man's.

After a time someone did buy the cabin and lived in it full-time. I always wondered what happened to the poor man who gave up on his dream cabin, but not enough to ever utter a peep about it.

Mom never was a jokester like Dad. She was a wild, fun-loving spirit whose laughter didn't come from tricking people. We could always get a laugh out of her just by being ourselves. We told stories that made fun of ourselves and her, and she was a spellbound listener and laugher. Her favorite stories were of her own absentmindedness; her own idiosyncrasies became hilarious when we relayed them back to her.

She willingly participated in screaming and dancing contests in the kitchen with us after dinner, and never minded our ludicrous skits and sacrilegious theatrical productions, which were performed with exhausting regularity. She was game for anything goofy, and we were full of opportunities.

She did, however, uncharacteristically enact the most outrageous and memorable practical joke of our lifetime.

We kids came home from school on April first to find that Mom had made us candy. Keep in mind it was April first and Mom had never ever in her natural-born life prepared an after-school treat for us. Not even a sliced apple. On this April first she made chocolate candies that looked like Russell Stover treats. She had gone to some trouble.

We were so eager and pleased to see the lovely plate of delights we forgot all about the date and didn't notice anything abnormal about her standing by the plate like Vanna White modeling a new car. We enthusiastically grabbed a treat and shoved it into our mouths. After a few chews we looked at each other quizzically. A few more chews and we stopped chewing. A few seconds later and we yelled, "It's soap!"

We split into pairs and ran for the two bathrooms. We spit the soap into the trash and grabbed washcloths and dug them into our mouths.

Someone bellowed, "Wash with water! It works!"

We took turns putting our mouths under the faucet to gargle and swish.

"Brush your teeth! It's the only way!" someone else screamed maniacally.

After twenty minutes of frothing and crying we emerged from the bathrooms, bedraggled and spent. We found Mom lying on the floor of the kitchen in the fetal position, still laughing so hard she couldn't get up or speak. Her face was wet with tears. We weren't mad at her. The trick was so cunning and perfect we could only respect her. I remember mostly feeling just so disappointed that the candy wasn't candy. It looked and smelled awfully good.

After Mom regained her composure, we sat around the table listening intently to her disclosure of the development of her joke. We were insanely jealous of her successful results and wanted to hear the play-by-play of every detail of her strategy. She'd found the trick in a book somewhere. She'd cut bars of Ivory soap into squares and heated up a sauce from chocolate chips which she poured over the squares. Then she let them cool and they were ready. We imagined the time and effort it took to cook up her scheme; we were nearly silent with reverence.

Just then we heard Dad come in.

Mom's face froze. Dad looked like he'd had a long, hard day at work. She did not want to add to his burden. Derick ran up to Dad with the plate of candy and said, "Look what Mom made!"

Dad didn't say a word. He picked up a candy and put it in his mouth. He bit down once. He stopped. He opened his mouth, pulled out the candy, and put it in the trash. We all stood silently, waiting for him to say something. Mom stood in the corner of the kitchen, her face white. Dad walked to the bathroom, and we heard water running. He came out, grabbed his paper, and sat down to read. Dad was always silent after work if he was in a bad mood, and he'd expect to be left alone. Even soap candy wasn't enough to get a word out of him.

Later on over dinner, we kids chattered on about the big joke. Dad didn't say anything, but we knew he admired the maneuver. Mom, the only one in the house who never really cared for fooling people, had bamboozled us. All of our schemes and conspiracies seemed juvenile and boring in comparison. We were proud of her.

Ugly Duckel-ing

Steamboat Springs Elementary

On my first day of school I saw two girls screaming and crying about their mothers leaving them in a strange place. I thought it the most preposterous thing I'd ever seen. Who in the world had decided to let these whiny babies start kindergarten? I couldn't have been more excited about Mom dropping me off somewhere.

School didn't disappoint me. I thought it was easy and fun. I got good grades, always had a few friends, was good at sports, and never got into trouble. I did have a heaping measure of insecurity, though.

For one, my clothes were not fancy, or even new. My parents loved a good bargain. Whether or not they actually needed to be as frugal as they were, I don't know. But they made an art of it. Although we window shopped at expensive May D and F in Denver, we never bought so much as a sock there. The actual purchases took place at garage sales,

Salvation Army, or Goodwill. I didn't complain because Mom didn't allow complaining, I wasn't used to anything different, and I got to pick out a whole lot of clothes—pretty much anything I wanted. I fared pretty well with my new/old outfits; I managed to put together some adequate ensembles with few or no stains and rips. The problem was that I was skinny. Starvation skinny. I could never find pants that fit properly. I had to cinch up every pair of paints with a belt, leaving bunched up fabric bulging between every belt loop. I spent all my school years self-consciously trying to pull my shirt over my lumpy pants. I was convinced that if I bought clothes at a real store like the other kids this wouldn't have been a problem, but I didn't realize that most of the other kids weren't starvation skinny.

When Mom's addiction to frugality was in full-gear there was a place to shop in Steamboat that was cheaper than Goodwill, and she called it the Trading Post. Most people called it the city dump.

"Why do you call it the Trading Post when you don't trade anything?" I asked her once.

"We call it the Trading Post so people don't hear you saying you got your toys and clothes at the dump."

"What's so bad about it?"

"Nothing. Just don't tell anyone. Ever."

I had no idea what was wrong with getting things at the dump. I thought it delightful. We would park our Kingswood Estate station wagon so as to be sufficiently tucked amid the mountains of garbage to be hidden from the view of passersby on Highway 40. (The SmartWool headquarters now occupies the ground where our joyful shopping sprees occurred.) Mom would shout "Don't get cut" as we all piled out and sprinted in all directions. The place was brimming with opportunity. What could possibly be more entertaining and exhilarating than searching for hidden treasure? Real hidden treasure!

That first dash out of the car was the best part about the experience; we had the grand idea that we might find something fantastic and rare. But inevitably that extraordinary booty eluded us. Ninety-nine percent of the time we pulled out items that were broken, sticky, stinky, or worse.

"Ah! Put that down! That's disgusting," we heard Mom yell over and over.

When we'd finally find something that was intact and reasonably easy to get clean we'd march over to Mom for inspection.

"No. That's broken."

"Just a little. Dad could fix this part."

"We're not bringing home a pile of broken crap for Dad to fix. No."

We didn't argue, and would scurry back to the mounds for more prospects.

In addition to the inconvenience of having to work very hard to find anything, there were a few other minor unpleasantries to contend with, not the least of which was the smell. The stench was always the same; a part of the place was always on fire, and the burning smell mixed with the odor of rotten food and decaying furniture. It was strong enough to produce watering eyes and frequent coughing. I didn't mind a single bit. By the time the Trading Post had become a regular habit, I'd come to associate its stench with the fine memories that came with it—satisfying family outings in which we all had a common goal, everyone got to participate with an unusual amount of autonomy, and there was always that thrilling promise of coming across the Mother Lode.

Although the dump seemed so full of possibility, our net proceeds never amounted to much. Mom usually walked away with things like a few pairs of old jeans or a half-working toaster. I think the most I ever came home with was a one-armed doll with a dirty dress that shrank into a microscopic ant garment after I washed it. I treasured the grubby girl longer than I should have, though, because she was hard-earned. Amazingly, after all the times we shopped at the dump we never cut ourselves or contracted any revolting diseases. I can officially say that it was good clean fun.

So in the end I didn't end up wearing Trading Post clothes to school. Goodwill and Salvation Army suited me up all right. There is little doubt that I would have been apprehensive about any clothes I'd worn anyway.

I did take with me a habit. For years I couldn't pass by a heap of discarded junk on the side of the road without slowing down to see what was in it. I'd get a thrill over the prospect that something might be in there that could be wonderful. I have an embarrassing amount of furniture in my home that I procured this way, and the pieces I hauled home happen to be some of my very best things. The Trading Post may not have paid off when I was a kid, but I learned something valuable from it.

In addition to my self-doubt concerning attire, I was painfully insecure about boys. Ever since I was four I could be considered boy-crazy. I day-dreamed way too much about whatever particular boy I had a crush on, but had the attitude that not ever, ever would he have anything to do with me. At far too young an age I was convinced I was doomed to a life of spinsterhood. Due to teasing from joking relatives, I had established that I was officially and unarguably the ugliest girl on Earth. Dad's silly name for Debi and me was the Sisty Uglers. Mom had been over-complimented for her beauty her whole life (which made her self-conscious), so she didn't want to burden her kids by commenting on her kids' appearance at all. Granny sometimes teased us saying we were homely. No one meant for me to believe I was truly ugly, but that's what I picked up. I didn't tell anyone because I didn't want someone to validate my assessment. From elementary into high school my ugly fixation troubled me, and I was blind to whether or not anyone else saw me that way.

Going through school boy-crazy and believing yourself hideously ugly is hard. Although I was able to focus on schoolwork, friends, and sports enough to do fine in those areas, it is surprising how much of my day was spent conjuring elaborate fantasies which involved me looking completely different than a blond-haired, green eyed, tall, skinny girl. In my dreams I was a short curvy gal with black, shiny hair, dark skin and brown eyes. And the boys adored me and would line up for a chance to date me. I had expensive, trendy clothes that fit me in the waist. I could laugh and smile at the boys like Stacy Venturi did, instead of looking at the ground. My dream world was a bittersweet place. It was pleasing, but I was positive no tiny part of it would ever come true. My secret haunted me all the way until high school, when I solved my problem by wearing too much make-up, which I believed covered up my repulsiveness.

My insecurity made my most embarrassing school moment a million times worse than it really was. In third grade I was on the playground when Jeff Fowel grabbed me by the arm and swung me around so that my buttoned shirt flew wide open in front of Scott Lorenz and Mark Kinney. I was mortified and relived the incident over and over in my mind for years, wishing I could turn back the clock and make it go away. I had no boobs whatsoever, but Scott and Mark teased me endlessly about it. The idea that I could shrug my shoulders and get over it was not an option. It haunted me. I wish someone would have taken me aside and said WHO CARES, but I was too embarrassed to tell anyone about it.

I actually showed a little bravery on the day of my most dramatic incident. We kids were standing in line for first-grade vaccinations in the nurse's office. In front of me in line was Danny Huspeth and Cathy Miller, good friends since early childhood. Danny stepped up for his shot, and as the needle entered his arm he screamed like a girl at the top of his lungs. Cathy fainted on the spot. Grownups ran hither and thither trying to contain the chaos while I stood still as a rock—not too happy about being next in line, but courageously ready to do my duty when everyone calmed down. Cathy's funny dad, Al, later gave me a cartoon of a lone duck standing on an island with a doomed look on his face. He said, "This is you after seeing Danny and Cathy in line in front of you." I could relate to it.

My most frightening moment was completely out of my control, like all most frightening moments. We had a playground contraption called "the rings." They were a sort of metal maypole with many long chains dangling from the top. The chains had a metal handle at the end to grab, and we would run with the handle around the spinning center pole and try to get lifted off the ground a bit. There were few days when a kid didn't get a bloody head from the rings; there is not a smidgeon of doubt that the rings would be forbidden these days. One day Penny Winograsky offered to push me on the rings, an act similar to pushing one on the merry-go-round. Since Penny and I didn't hang out much, I was excited to get to play with a new friend. I was pleasantly surprised that she was as strong as a grown man (it seemed) and could get me way off the ground right away. In no time I was flying higher than I ever had on the rings—over the heads of everyone. As I passed her on the third go round she continued to push me higher, and soon my skinny body was completely horizontal and whipping around in a circle. A small crowd gathered, amazed at how high I was, and Penny laughed and bragged about how she'd gotten me that way. It wasn't long before I realized that I wasn't slowing down or getting lower, and my hands were getting sweaty. My face changed from glee to horror, and I began screaming at Penny to stop pushing me. She didn't catch on. She laughed, proud of her pushing prowess, oblivious to my S.O.S. call, and kept on shoving me as I went around. She was just having fun, but from my terrified, slippery-handed, spinning and flying point of view, Penny looked like the evil laughing clown in the movies who slices up people in the fun house. As I would pass over her cackling head I'd howl and plead for her to stop. She just laughed harder. I knew I was going to have to let go. I chose a spot where there were no people, closed my eyes, and let lose.

The pain was instant and awful. I landed on pavement. I screamed and cried as I got up and saw blood all over the place. Penny's face changed real fast. She looked as white as I was. She and another girl ran over and started helping me toward the nurse's office. I screamed and screamed. I don't remember how many body parts were skinned, but it was enough for a lot of kids to shudder as we passed them, hobbling to the school. No teacher came to help. The playground monitors were few and far between then. I left a red trail to the nurse's office, but got there eventually. Penny sat by my bedside and smiled and told jokes and was as nice as anyone I've ever seen. I know she felt bad, and I hate to say it, but I think the whole incident might have been worth it to me at the time just to have her act like that toward me.

By the time I got out of school that day I was limping a little and half-covered in gauze pads, but running around as usual and thoroughly enjoying the attention. Penny and others relayed the incident to everyone, so I got pats on the back and "are you OKs," which made the event even more worth it. I think the memory would have actually turned into a good one if it hadn't been for the haunting image of flying in terror over Penny's yowling face. The poor girl had no idea how I imagined her for years to come.

The most shocking moment of childhood was seeing Jeanette Green and Judd Jacobs making out under the slide. I was in second grade and they were in third! They were lying down, locked in an embrace that I hadn't even seen grownups participate in. Other kids just walked around as if nothing was happening; I couldn't understand why no one thought this a bit odd, to say the least. I'm even more shocked now that I'm in my 40s and know how innocent a third grader should be.

My biggest failure (besides the short-sheet incident) happened at the home of Super Dooper Mrs. Hooper's house. Mom invented the name for the woman who babysat us pretty often from the time we were toddlers. Super Dooper and her six kids (all with red hair and names that started with R) lived in a house that was, I swear, no more than 500 square feet. It looked like a shed. Her back yard was no bigger than a small bedroom, and had no grass—only dirt, surrounded by a chain-link fence. She not only babysat the four Duckels kids, but twelve to fifteen other neighborhood kids. This was obviously a time before daycare laws were introduced to our part of the world. Needless to say, Super Dooper was never in a good mood, and none of us received a lick of attention. As a small child I remember having juice spills on my shirt, covering my ears to block out the sound of screaming babies, plugging my nose to block out the smell of dirty diapers, and trying to find a few square feet of space to myself so I could draw.

By the time I was in fourth grade I didn't go to Super Dooper's to be babysat. I was old enough to become a member of 4H, and she was the leader. Most of my girl classmates at school chose one of two different after-school clubs— Girl Scouts or 4H. Cute and popular Cathy McGill and Kristen Smith were in Girl Scouts. It was my basic understanding that I was more of a 4H kind of girl. 4H was generally considered for farm kids. Raising livestock, cooking, sewing, and other pursuits were learned, and competitions for ribbons were held at county and state fairs. I couldn't raise livestock because we lived in town, so I learned sewing. At least I tried.

After school, on Super Dooper's sewing machine, I tried to sew straight seams while shrieking children ran pell-mell by me, rivers of snot trailing through the dirt on their face from their noses straight into their mouths. Super Dooper would try to explain sewing patterns to me, but I don't remember her ever finishing a sentence without having to interrupt to bawl out a kid for pooping their pants or screaming too loud. I tried to sit real close to Ruby Moser, another 4H member, and talk while we sewed our hems, but the distractions proved too much. We could barely hear each other, and all we really wanted to talk about was how crazy that place was.

When it was time to display our wares at the Routt County Fair, I knew my skirt and matching jacket were a pitiful sight. My elastic waistband flipped over once or twice inside its tube, the bottoms of the hems were crooked, and my lapels were uneven. Those dang Stetson girls, from another 4H group, had made six-piece matching ensembles that looked factory-made. They got fat, shiny purple ribbons. I got a little white ribbon. This was a nice consolation ribbon that said Third Place, but really meant Last Place.

I was always determined to be the best. If I were going to try anything, I was going to do it well. I was infuriated at myself for being so bad at sewing! My last try at getting it right was a simple red poncho with one seam, to be my entry for the Colorado State Fair. With the thunderous commotion of Super Dooper's Wild Kingdom in the background, I tried to muster every bit of concentration I had to get that poncho acceptable for the fair. I ripped out the crooked seam ten times. Super Dooper would look it over every time and shake her head. We both knew the seam meandered like a sidewinder. I think she felt sorry for me while I ripped out the ninth uneven seam. She patted my shoulders. Finally, on the eleventh try, she leaned over my sewing machine and said, "That looks perfect." It was as crooked as all the ones before. I knew what she meant was, "Hang it up, Dori." I was so happy to stop, but it was the first time that I had to face that I was just not good at something and I wouldn't be, no matter how hard I tried. I felt like a failure for a few hours, but backing out of State Fair was an enormous relief. I wore my poncho to school for years, and nobody ever said anything about my wandering seam.

The enforcers of daycare laws eventually shut Super Dooper Mrs. Hooper down. From then on you only saw red-haired kids in her yard, with names that began with R.

My most romantic incident would be considered unremarkable to anyone with a little confidence, but since I was the Ugliest Girl on Earth I could get elated over the slightest bit of attention.

I had an inkling that David Ethridge might have had an eye on me in Mrs. Whiteman's third-grade class. I still don't know if this is true, but I caught him looking at me a few times, and he was fairly sweet to me. I only narrowly believed that he really did like me, and mostly pondered what in the world he found attractive about me, if he even did find me attractive, which he probably didn't anyway. I didn't waste my hopes on him. I continued having my crush on John Gittleson, who didn't know I existed. This was a sure way to never have to deal with boys at all, because if I picked someone who knew I existed, I faced the horrifying prospect of finding out for certain that no one would ever like me. Remaining invisible was the safest bet. It all seemed very logical to me.

In Mrs. Whiteman's class, we all took turns at demonstrating a science experiment, and our presentations were encouraged to be as simple as possible. (I illustrated how one's hand turns white when one holds it above the head because of gravity and blood and so forth.) David Ethridge got up to take his turn on his assigned day and brought a large bowl of water, some black pepper, and a bar of soap up to the teacher's desk. He was ready to do his demonstration, but Mrs. Whiteman looked concerned and said, "Oh dear. No one's going to be able to see the trick because the bowl can't be tipped up. I don't want the whole class clamoring around my desk, so why don't you pick two people to come up and see?"

David picked two boys.

"Well, one boy is fine, but I think a girl should get to see, too. Pick a girl, David."

Without a moment's hesitation David Ethridge said, "Dori Duckels."

My face grew beet red. I knew everyone watched me as I walked up to the front of the room, so I tried to act relaxed. I doubt I hid my feelings. I felt honored, embarrassed, and slightly giddy.

David began his simple trick while Mrs. Whiteman, the boy, and I crowded around the bowl. He sprinkled black pepper on the surface of the water, and then touched the bar of soap to the water in the center of the pepper sprinkles. The pepper immediately darted away.

That was it. Something to do with the film of soap spreading across the water surface. It was an interesting sight, and the boy and I said wow. The rest of the class complained that they couldn't come up and see, and Mrs. Whiteman told them in her super nice way to shut up. She then explained what the trick was about. Meanwhile I stood next to David and didn't hear anything. David's soft, warm hand was touching mine. He may not have known it, or maybe he was doing it on purpose. I stood dead still, not moving my hand, hoping to make the moment last as long as possible. Mrs. Whiteman droned on about the experiment— much longer than the simple trick warranted, and I considered it good luck. David didn't move and I didn't move and no one noticed for what seemed like forever. Then it was over.

We sat down and that was it. For the rest of third grade, David still glanced my way occasionally and I still wondered if he really liked me, if anyone possibly could. But I always got a funny feeling in my stomach when I thought about him calling out my name so quickly. I wouldn't let myself dwell too long on the hand-touching thing. I tried to convince myself that he just didn't notice. But I was never really sure.

Steamboat Springs Junior High

Junior High started in sixth grade. It was a dark time. Puberty magnified my insecurity a thousand fold, and every waking moment seemed to be torture. I was almost to my full height (nearly 6 feet) at the time and weighed 110 pounds. I looked like a concentration camp victim. I tried to gain weight by regularly eating a pound of cheese in one sitting, but nothing happened. I once talked my best friends, Cathy Miller and Tracy Perryman, into telling Davin Vanatta that I liked him. I'd had an aching crush on him for years. Tracy came back to report his distressing reply. "She's too skinny." I wished I could double my cheese intake, but wolfing down a pound was already pushing it.

I had no boobs and wore silly granny glasses that I'd picked out in third grade. To make everything worse, I got straight A pluses. I ascertained that no boy wanted anything to do with a smart girl. Most of my time was spent day dreaming about being pretty and popular, getting Cs, and having non-Goodwill clothes. As I said, it was a dark time.

Hormones mean crazy chemicals running around your brain, and Junior High felt like a bad acid trip. But peeping through the haze of those unhappy times were some shining moments with my girlfriends. I sat in the back row of classes with Cathy and Tracy, drawing pretty ladies and birds, and still got straight As. With Katie Lee, Jill Wood, and

Erin Lewis I hung out in our Fish Creek neighborhood. We aspired to be rebellious teen-agers, but our antics amounted to nothing more than irreverent talk, trying on make-up, sneaky laughter, and some creative pre-teen mischief. A bright spot in junior high was being befriended by Cathy McGill and Jolene Stetson—popular, nice, and smart girls who, to be honest, I think, felt sorry for me. They took me under their wing and let me hang out with them. Whether they realized it or not, their charity put a dent in my monumental self-loathing, and may have paved the way for the better times that awaited me in high school.

One tale of junior high must be told. Darla Dink (not her real name) was my locker mate, because our names started with a D. Darla and I got along well. We each brought our lunch to school daily, and kept them on our separate shelves. Not too long after our lockers were assigned, I noticed that dessert items were coming up missing from my lunch sack. I mentioned it to Darla a couple of times, and she politely said she was sorry, and she'd stop taking my food, but my generic version of Oreos must have been too hard to resist. My dessert kept disappearing. If it weren't for the fact that I was trying to gain weight, I wouldn't have cared that much, but I needed every last fattening calorie I could get. I told Mom. Mom felt sorry for me, losing my dessert, and for Darla, who couldn't stop herself in a bad habit. Thinking she could effectively solve our problem with a quick and easy solution, Mom came up with an attention-grabbing plan.

She must have become a little bold after her chocolate soap trick. She went shopping and came home with some Russell Stover chocolates with cherries inside, a syringe, and some rubbing alcohol. She injected the alcohol into the candies and put them back into their foil wrapper.

"There. That ought to work," she said.

"Mom! What if she dies?"

"It's alcohol! People drink it everyday."

I went to school the next day with my secret contaminated delicacy. I was nervous. Normally, when I was involved in a tricky scheme to fool someone, I was woozy with delight, but this deception involved someone outside our family. I wasn't sure how other folks reacted to ingenious diabolical conspiracies aimed at them. I left my lunch sack on its shelf in the locker, and during the half-hour before school started, told a few friends about my prank. There was no giggling on our parts. We discussed the plan as if it were a business deal: going over the pros and cons, listing the social repercussions, contemplating the scientific effects of rubbing alcohol on the human body, pondering the ethics of it all. I was a little sick from all my second thoughts. The bell rang and off we went to our classes.

After first period I returned to my locker to find Darla waiting for me. She'd heard. Word had spread.

"Did you really do it?" she said.

"Yes," I said, not knowing what to expect from her.

"Well, I won't take any more food from you." She was mad, and told me I didn't have to take it that far.

"O.K." I said. "I'm sorry." I waited for something else to be said, but that was it. Things went back to normal pretty quickly, but Darla never took my dessert again. Soon after, we got along as well as before. Mom's plan had worked, indirectly. The crazy thing is, looking back, that no one in the situation voiced to me any suggestion that the event was the slightest bit outlandish. No parents filing a lawsuit, no teachers forming a tribunal, no kids spreading devastating rumors, no local or national news team blowing it out of proportion. Those were the days.

Steamboat Springs High School

As I mentioned before, I pulled myself out of the
miserable stupor of Junior High in my freshman year of
High School by wearing too much make-up to cover my
perceived ugliness. I believed people could now look me in
the eye without noticing how revolting I was. Although I took
seriously my attempts to be more attractive, I was sure the
boys did not. I was still super tall and skinny and hung out
with smart girls. I needed to fix that. When hanging out in
the halls I slouched as much as I could to try to fit in. And in
a shameful act of betrayal and disloyalty, I disowned Cathy
Miller and Tracy Perryman, my much-loved-since-early-
childhood smart friends. I started hanging out with the cute,
popular, cheerleader-type girls. My smart friends were hurt
and let me know. I shrugged. I very seriously decided that
my misery would be fixed if I could just fit in with the cool
kids.

The popular girls wondered what this gangly nerd
girl was doing on the periphery of their hang-out circles, but
with tenacity I kept poking my head in and making
comments until they started including me in their activities. I
did it for a while. Acted like a cool girl. It wasn't hard. I had
to laugh at their jokes and learn how to make similar ones,
find interest in the things they did (gossip and boys) and
make efforts to get together with one or two of them outside
of school so I could talk and laugh about it back at school in
front of the other girls.

I did it for maybe a year, but it got boring, and
eventually I drifted back to being friends with girls I could be
myself around. (They forgave me instantly.) I didn't stop

wearing too much make-up, but not being my goofy old self was too much to ask.

Art was my favorite subject since kindergarten, and in high-school art class was the highlight of my week. I had several teachers that I liked at Steamboat High, but Tom Wither, our art teacher, was my idol. He was funny and irreverent, and he treated us kids like we were his good friends. We called him Tee Dub for short. He was passionate and laid back at the same time. He dressed hip, and listened to cool music. He was encouraging, and respectful of all students' artwork. He assigned us interesting projects. I wondered why everyone on Earth wouldn't want to be in art class every day, all day.

Perhaps I loved his class because I excelled at art and I related to Tee Dub's artistic sensibility, one that I would eventually take on and be surrounded with for good. Whatever the reason, Tee Dub's class was my sanctuary, my church. This was where I felt truly at home.

I saw Tee Dub mad only once. And he was way mad. Our assignment for the week was to do a self-portrait in watercolors, using bright, contrasting colors. I worked very hard on my piece (as usual) and came up with a fine-looking likeness of myself with a yellow face and blue hair. I was quite happy with it when we turned our work in at the end of class one day, and I could tell Tee Dub liked it, too. When we returned for class again, Tee Dub had laid everyone's work out on tables for us to see, and our grades were on little pieces of paper, attached with a paper clip. I walked past the bright red, green, purple and orange faces: some wild and primitive, others straight and tidy. I stopped dead in my tracks when I got to mine. There, under my pleasant, multi-colored countenance was the word Bitch, written in Magic

Marker. Blood rushed to my face. Being called a name was bad enough, but ruining my art—now that was unthinkable. I was mortified.

Tee Dub hadn't seen it yet. My face red and my heart beating, I walked over to his desk and told him to come look. He walked over to the paintings in his usual jovial manner, until he looked down at my watercolor. I'd rarely ever seen him without a smile, so the look that formed on his face was quite alarming. Boy, was he mad. He shouted at the class for a few minutes, but it was, of course, futile to try and find the culprit. It could have been done by anyone from any class. He stopped yelling and began cussing under his breath while looking at my piece. He eventually wandered back over to his desk to teach, but he was clearly solemn and subdued the rest of class. I was grateful that his reaction mirrored mine; it validated how violated I felt.

During class I mulled over possible suspects—someone I knew who hated me—but came up with no obvious enemies to blame. It felt weird and troubling to think someone out there disliked me that much. But much more serious to me was the defamation of a work of art. This person was foul—an immoral and malevolent person! I decided I'd better watch my back; I had a real sicko on my bad side.

After art class my very good friends Lorrie Taylor and Lauren DeRosa surrounded me, wanting to cheer me up, threatening to dismember whoever did it, and asked who I thought it was. I told them I was stumped, but without delay, changed the conversation to the real matter at hand: Who could stoop so low as to wreck someone else's artwork? They didn't get it. They laughed as if it were a joke, I thanked them for being sweeties, and within a minute or so they were off to their next class.

Before getting off to my next class, I turned around and saw Tee Dub through the glass of the closed door to the art room. He was standing over my watercolor, his arms and hands limp by his side, his head low, his profile with no expression. I knew I shared something with my teacher, a way of seeing things that was a little different. I didn't know then that my different way of seeing things would form the foundation for most of my life choices from high-school on. I did know then a really important thing, one that many artistic kids need to know in the worst way, especially in high-school. I was not alone.

Tee Dub was my favorite teacher, and Miss Jalp was not. (I've changed her name in case she might come after me with a bomb; you'll see why soon enough.) When school started, Miss Jalp (a heavyset woman with a decidedly masculine demeanor) came across as a little peculiar, but not strange enough to mention to someone after class. A few of us made comments to each other that she seemed to be trying too hard to get us to like her. She taught U. S. History in a style that could be called schizophrenic vaudevillian. Over-exaggerated facial expressions, frivolous laughter after listing the presidents in a monotone voice, and long, uncomfortable silences marked her weird style. She took long strides and swung her arms as she paced back and forth across the front of the room, giving details of the trenches in World War I with a silly grin on her face. But for all her antics, she never managed to communicate a stitch of information that stuck in our heads. To be sure, we learned nothing.

Miss Jalp's first test was as odd as her lessons. We spent half our time trying to make out her handwritten, mimeographed pages, and the other half puzzling over questions that distantly related (maybe) to her perplexing daily floor shows. Rob Hall sat next to me in Miss Jalp's class, and we looked at each other and shrugged. When our tests were handed back Miss Jalp expressed dismay. She marched up and down the rows of desks, flustered, making comments about how unusual it was that an entire class of kids could get Ds and Fs. Rob and I were normally A students, so her dismay couldn't have been much worse than ours.

As the weeks went by, Miss Jalp's behavior gradually grew more bizarre. Her curious lectures became more erratic and extreme, her moods unreliable. One day she'd exhibit a form of manic jolliness, relaying only tiny bits of historical information and lots of stories about her personal life, which included a little too much information about her "man-friends." The next day she'd look as if her body was made of lead. Gloomy and gray, she'd absently list some facts from the history book and dismiss us early. Her temper was frightening. Unpredictably, on any given day, she'd lash out at a student for being disrespectful, or for not getting a question right. Her face would turn red, and she'd march up to the student's seat and yell in his face. (I never saw it happen to a girl.)

We students definitely started talking about her outside class. We told other teachers, we told other students, and we talked among ourselves. We didn't have Oprah telling us to be understanding of those with mental illness. We didn't have Oprah telling us that mental illness existed. This woman was crazy, and it made one heck of a story!

Miss Jalp was not only a history teacher. She was also the assistant gymnastics coach. I was not a gymnast (my long skinny arms could never hold up a back-handspring) but many of my friends were on the team. I heard stories from them about how volatile she was during practice and meets. All stories circulated easily and speedily through our small-town school, and this story had enough juicy ingredients to get it stirred around faster than usual. The rumors got back to Miss Jalp.

One day Rob and I sat near the front of the room, waiting for class to start, and wondering why Miss Jalp was fifteen minutes late. We were deliberating over whether or not we should just leave when we heard the classroom door slam so loud it shook the whole corridor. After nearly swallowing our tongues from shock, we watched, wide-eyed, as Miss Jalp came bounding to the front of the room—blonde hair flapping and feet stomping—her face scarlet and scrunched. She let us have it. She yelled profanities at us for quite awhile, gave us a massive assignment from the book, and told us we were having a test the next day. Then she told us to get out.

The days when she'd release us early were not easy on us. We weren't ever allowed to roam the halls between classes, so we had to make ourselves invisible until the bell rang for the next class. We got good at it, using an age-old Steamboat High hiding place—the woodsy area down by Spring Creek, near the school. We called it Hooterville, because that's where the freaks went to smoke dope. It was a good place to take a little break if the weather wasn't too bad.

That day a few of us didn't walk, we ran down to Hooterville, because Miss Jalp's disagreeable episode had left us feeling devious and wayward. As I plowed through the thicket toward the creek, my arm got scratched on a branch and bled. It wasn't enough to cause alarm, so we sat on the pot-smoker logs, dazed and shook-up, wondering what was going to happen next with Miss Jalp. I dabbed my bloody arm with my sleeve until it stopped.

The next day we apprehensively walked into Miss Jalp's class. She was there waiting for us with a stack of tests to hand out, a big smile on her face. Rob and I had put some effort into studying the night before, but there was too much to get through without staying up late, and we had no previous instruction that prepared us for her assignment. I cringed as she started handing out tests; I half-expected her to strike someone. As she approached each desk she had a wide, frenzied smile that was impossible to interpret.

We began our tests. Right away, Miss Jalp walked up to a boy, took his pen, and filled in one of the answers for him. He said, "Thanks," and she beamed and said, "Sure, anyone else?" Two kids tentatively raised their hands, and she walked over and answered their questions for them. Rob and I looked at each other. Miss Jalp saw us and said, "Go ahead, you can help each other." Within minutes the whole class was cheating off each other, out loud. After a while kids were shouting answers across the room. Miss Jalp was turning us all bonkers!

We left class that day with As on our weird test. Creepy As. Miss Jalp patted our backs as we walked out the door. And that was the last we ever saw of her.

For a few days after that, we had a substitute, until our principal informed us that Miss Jalp had disappeared, and had left not a single shred of paper that showed any work we'd done that term. She was gone, but had left one thing of grave importance: a bomb threat, directed at the gymnastics team, and designated to take place during their upcoming tournament. As usual, our girls' gymnastics team, led by the incredibly bendy Terry Patterson, was headed to the state championships, and was almost certain to take first place. Several of my friends, including Katie Lee, Kathy Ramunno, and Melanie Sprengle were on the team, so I heard daily reports of the precautions the team was taking to protect the girls. Perhaps if they weren't the best team in the state they would have cancelled their trip. Frannie, the gymnastics and track coach, had to make sure the team had a police escort throughout their expedition. The girls ended up taking state as expected, and they still have all their body parts to prove that Miss Jalp's threats came to nothing.

Without records of any kind to prove we'd even taken a class, the powers that be thought long and hard about how to deal with classrooms full of kids with a lost semester. They ultimately came up with a rotten solution, in our opinion, which required Miss Jalp's former students to take the U.S. History final given by Mr. McEvilly, reputed to be a very hard teacher. By the time they'd come up with a plan, we had a couple nights to study. In our most serious manner we explained that Miss Jalp had taught us nothing. The principal claimed the school had no other choice unless we wanted to flunk. Our only consolation was that they would grade on a curve, comparing only Miss Jalp's students. This meant we had a chance, but were competing with each other.

Preparing for McEvilley's test was the only time in my life when I pulled a real all-nighter for schoolwork. We were given a study guide that was as thick as a dictionary. I saw the sun come up while still memorizing the points of the New Deal. Until I sat down to take the test I used every scrap of brain concentration to keep those facts and dates in my head. I got through the final pretty quickly and was not dissatisfied with how I'd done. I instantly allowed all the information to drift back to the ether so I could breath freely again. Both Rob and I ended up getting a B. I wondered who the jerk was that got an A and spoiled it for us, but considering the state of affairs, I didn't have much to complain about.

Miss Jalp left me with more ways to remember her than she will ever know. I still have a scar on my left arm where I got scratched up in Hooterville. And she circuitously gave me a love of history that continues today. After McEvilley's test, I knew I'd remember nothing except for a few names of people or ideas with no definitions attached, i.e. the New Deal (whatever that was) happened in the 20th century. I left high school feeling cheated. I tried to catch up by taking a college course in Western Civilization that stuffed my brain (again) with names and dates and kings, kings, kings, but never a good grasp on What Happened. So after college I checked out historical biographies by the garbage sack-full from the juvenile section of the public library wherever I lived. I learned history through stories of people, and it came together in a fun, fascinating, easy picture. It was like watching an unbelievable, spellbinding movie. It still is.

No one that I know ever heard from Miss Jalp again.

Ninety kids made up the class of '81, and plenty of them had been my friends at one time or another since we were toddlers. We'd spent so much of our lives together we were almost like siblings. Decades after I left high school I still had frequent dreams about my Steamboat friends—as often as I did my own family.

High school can be a pressure-cooker of hormones and high drama, and, like most everyone, I had cruel days when I thought I was a loser and the whole world hated me. Other days I thought everyone else was a loser and I hated the whole world. My good buddies never ever failed to be there for me. They patted me and said "he's an asshole anyway" when my heart was broken by an unrequited crush, ran to get tampons in emergency situations, put aloe on my sunburns, and said "at least you played great" when we lost a game. We stuffed ourselves with candy, turned up Van Halen and Queen too loud, laughed about everything in the world, danced constantly, screamed like banshees for no reason, and skipped and held hands when we were supposed to be way too old for it.

Nudity excited us. We sunbathed topless on the hoods of the school buses (and got caught), swam nude in a pool in Meeker after a wrestling tournament (and got caught), and mooned the town of Craig from our school bus (and got in big trouble; more about that later). After all the eye-rolling as a child with Dawn and Gretchen Hippy-Chick at the Hot Springs, I turned out just like them.

Sometimes we flaunted our sports ribbons and trophies for the other teams, other times we walked arm in arm back to the locker room with tired, straight faces. We shared hot potatoes at cold football games, passing it around and sticking in our coat. For wrestling matches we memorized absurd cheers that probably embarrassed the wrestlers more than it helped. We lost our voices from shrieking for hours straight at basketball games against Glenwood Springs. We were both fierce competitors and immature troublemakers at track meets.

When we were having fun we knew of only one moment—the silly, unimportant, I-hope-no-one-else-is-watching moment we were in. Those moments, however seemingly insignificant, strung together to form a powerful charm that spat on the head (or farted in the general direction) of my insecurity, academic stress, and those damn hormones. High school wasn't a total joy ride, but I am lucky to be able to say it was probably more fun that it was poopy, thanks to my friends.

By the end of high school I stopped believing I was ugly altogether. I've found in more recent years that many people, whether they were from Steamboat or not, had overblown insecurity issues when they were younger. I've also discovered that I was not seen by most of my schoolmates as pitiful and unattractive. Apparently there were a few boys who liked me from afar, but were as afraid to voice it as I would have been. Today I get to look back at my school years and re-live those memories as if I knew the truth then: except for slipping drug-laced candy to unsuspecting children, I was a fairly normal girl.

Butts are for Boxing

All the Duckels kids were good athletes, and all the sports in which we competed were important to us. By the time we graduated from high school, the four of us had broken school sports records, new records, some which ended up holding for over 20 years. But thanks to my Dad's maniacal enthusiasm for the sport, basketball was kingdaddy of our home. Dad had been a star player on the Steamboat High team and had gone on to play for the CSU Aggies in Fort Collins. As a kid he was exceptionally shy and quiet, but basketball thrust him into the limelight where, without having to utter a word, he could shine. I have always been mesmerized by the movie Hoosiers because it portrayed exactly the way I picture Dad's golden years of a small town high-school basketball team in the 50s. He even looked just like the star player in the movie.

Returning to Steamboat after college, Dad played on city leagues for fun, but I think it frustrated him to play on teams that weren't taken very seriously. He probably couldn't wait until his kids were old enough to make free-throws. His ultimate dream would have been to father five boys, all over 6' 4", so he could reign over his own team.

He often spoke with eagerness and veneration of just such a legend—a family from a tiny town in eastern Colorado with five towering boys, all first-rate basketball players. Their town was so small that the amazing five made up the entire team. Dad said they ended up beating one of the biggest schools in Colorado in the state championships and all went on to kick butt in good colleges. I couldn't count all the times Dad told us that story, or the times we asked him to "tell us that one again about the basketball family." We used any means necessary to get him to spill a few words. Basketball stories were the easiest way to get him talking, and they usually came along with one of his infrequent smiles. A question about the archaic granny shot, a reference to Larry Bird, or the mere mention of the state of Indiana could get him going.

Long soliloquies involving his favorite legend started like this:

"Hey Derick? Who's the best basketball player that ever lived?"

"Michael Jordan."

"Nope. It's Bill Russell."

Derick always guessed Michael Jordan and Dad always disagreed. And on Dad would go about Bill Russell.

On one of our Sunday evening drives in the summer Debi, Derick, and I were sitting up front in Dad's pickup and staring at the dirt road in front of us. Maybe we'd glance over at the Yampa River alongside the road or stare up at majestic Mt. Werner in the distance. Dad was too busy singing "Oh Suzanna" under his breath to notice the giggly whispers that began among the three of us. We were on River Road just past the neighborhood of Brooklyn, when I shouted, "Look! There's a basketball in the bushes!"

Dad slammed on the breaks hard enough to throw us all against the dash and send the rear of the pickup sliding to one side. Only a basketball could have provoked such a response. Unaware of the dramatic stop, he peered into the bushes on the side of the hill with his best hunter vision.

The three of us yelled, "Monkeys always look!"

Dad, the true lover of practical jokes, smiled, and in true form, said "Hmmm" and drove on. Debi and I looked at each other with a knowing smile. We had fooled him good, and he knew it.

The first part of Dad's ultimate dream of a basketball-playing family came true. We are all tall. Debi and I, at 5'11," were among the tallest girls in our classes and Derick, although only 6'1," boasted a soaring 41" vertical jump at his peak—a feat difficult for even professional basketball players. Dana is 5'9" and what she lacked in stature she more than made up for in sheer aggression on the court.

As we kids entered high school one by one, Dad's interest in forming us into models of basketball-playing perfection raised to full tilt. During basketball season we were treated like prize racehorses before the Kentucky Derby. Most of the school year we had to find our way home from whatever extracurricular activity we partook in. After practice for the school musical I wouldn't even think of calling for a ride, even if it wasn't over until 11:30. I'd hitchhike home, knowing that if I called for a ride I'd hear a groggy, "Can't you find a ride from someone else?" During basketball season we received rides home from school after practice. On nights when basketball practice didn't get over until 7 or 7:30—and Dad would have by then eaten his dinner and sunk into his newspaper—we would call from school to hear the eager response, "I'll be right down there!"

During the season, we'd be treated to long conversations over dinner, all focused on us. "Us" meant our basketball abilities, our coach's methods, our practice and game schedule, and our free throw and rebound averages. Outside of basketball season, dinner was a quiet affair for Dad. As always, he rarely spoke, and if Mom hadn't long ago laid down the law about not watching television during dinner, we would have been left out in favor of Ward Lucas and Reynelda Muse on Channel 4 News. Every once in a while, especially near election time, we'd hear a lecture about the stupid Democrats, but usually he'd try to tune out us blabbermouth kids, all spilling tales of our day at school or teasing each other about this or that love interest.

After dinner during B-ball season, it was not uncommon for Dad to take one of us aside and give us pointers, see how our ball-handling skills were shaping up, and even shoot a few hoops outside in the dark. Of course Steamboat resembles the Arctic Circle during basketball season, so all of these after-dinner scrimmages required gloves, snow boots, hats, and the shoveling of the driveway under the basket. Our driveway was never paved, so dribbling was a real effort on a gravel surface covered with chunky ice and snow. I never took well to the nighttime outdoor training sessions, but Debi, Derick, and Dana put up with them surprisingly well. From a nearby window, snuggled in slippers and blankets, Mom and I would observe their practices—their breath as visible as a steam engine's smoke, the bright lights above the garage reflecting on the snowflakes that swirled around them, the clunk against the backboard that shook the house windows.

As for the tips we received, they usually involved some illegal way to disconcert the other team and not get caught by the ref. He taught us to pull the other girls pants down, ram them with our rear end, elbow them, say rude things in their ears, nudge them backwards until they fell down; all without looking like we were fouling. Off the court, this kind of behavior would qualify as merely funny to Dad, but on court these tactics were a crucial ingredient of fundamental basketball skills.

We considered Dad's basketball advice as important, if not more important, than that of our coaches at school. But Coach Shikles did give one bit of counsel that remained our favorite basketball adage forever after. Frustrated after a long practice with prissy girls who wouldn't get aggressive enough, Coach said, "Ladies! The reason God gave women big butts is so they can box people out under the basket!" On the snowy drive home from practice in Dad's hot pickup, I told him Coach Shikles's words of wisdom. Dad laughed *out loud* (I nearly fell out of the truck with shock to hear it), and he drove all the way home with a smile on his face. I never forgot to repeat the adage on a regular basis—in hopes of a smile—and I always got one.

The very best thing about Dad during the season was his behavior during our basketball games. He never missed a game if he could help it, and that meant traveling to the nearest towns that we competed against, hours away. Our other teammates couldn't believe our Dad would attend even Rangeley games—a fantastically boring three-hour drive from Steamboat. Whether at away or home games, this was the *only* time Dad would emerge from his quiet world. He would become a screaming, fight-picking, fist-shaking madman. Everyone in the stands, and even us players in the middle of a game could distinguish my Dad's high-pitched screaming at a ref's bad call. To Dad, there were a lot of bad calls.

"Get your hair out of your eyes, ref," he'd yell at the official with a crew cut. "What are you doing out there? Scooping ice cream? This isn't scooping Haagen Daas, you know!"

On the off-chance that a traveling call would be mistaken: "Traveling? What do mean traveling? I'll show you traveling! I'll travel down there and pull your head out!"

If the other team was too aggressive: "What are you watching out there, ref? Your fingernails? She's getting beat up under the basket! What do they have to do to get you to call it? Ride her like a monkey?"

And his most frequently used attack: "Get yourself some new glasses, ref! Your prescription's gone bad!"

The madder Dad got at the refs, the higher his voice got and the more physical he became. If our team was losing on account of bad calls, he would be on his feet, waving his arms, on the verge of obscenities. God help anyone in the stands who might tell him to calm down. After one game a fellow player said, "I think your Dad almost got in a fight with Mr. Stevens, Dori."

"How do you know?"

"My Dad said something about your Dad going crazy at the refs, and when Mr. Stevens told him to settle down, he turned around and starting yelling at him."

"What did he say?"

"My Dad wouldn't say, but it wasn't good I don't think."

I asked Dad about it but he shrugged it off as no big deal. He had a right to make noise just like everyone else. (I have to admit, I was pretty mad at the call, too. Winna Arroyo got a technical foul for saying "What a bummer" from the bench.)

My Dad and I did have one major disagreement concerning basketball—the old Converse High Top Controversy. In Dad's glory days, he and all his teammates wore Converse's Chuck Taylor model—the simple, flat-soled, canvas basketball shoe that eventually became more popular with punk-rockers and artists than sportheads. In the mid 70's, when I first tried out for the team, padded leather high tops with bouncy soles had just become available and were, for good reason, the sound choice of basketball players everywhere. Not only were Chuck Taylors incredibly nerdy at the time, they were inferior in every way as basketball shoes. Dad insisted I wear them. "If they were good enough for me. . . ." I argued and pleaded and offered to pay the extra money out of my own pocket, but Dad insisted that Chuck Taylors were the best basketball shoes you could own. I wore them and hated them. Debi, Derick, and Dana fought the good fight against Chuck Taylor, too, and one of them eventually wore him down and was allowed to wear Nike Air.
Ironically I own two pairs now, and although I still insist there are better basketball shoes out there, Chuck Taylor eventually won my heart as kick-around shoes just because they are a part of my past, right or wrong. And my siblings and I can always look at them and say, "Dad and his Converse High Tops."

As a player I never thought I was all that good. To Dad I had the potential to become the next champion of the world. Never, ever, ever did he say one bad word about my basketball abilities. I could do no wrong. If I had a terrible game, he'd only tell me about all the good things I did and gently suggest a few pointers that might help me next time. If I had a great game he'd rave about my performance for days.

Truthfully, I was a terrible ball-handler. I almost never allowed myself to dribble during a game for fear it would bounce off my foot and fly out of bounds, or be snatched by the other team. Everyone thought I was a great team player because the minute I got the ball I'd pass it to someone else. I did this only so I wouldn't screw up when I had the ball. As the tallest player on the team I always played the position of center, which, on a small-town girl's basketball team, meant that my only requirement was to wait for the ball to be thrown to me, and shoot—or pass it along, if I didn't have a shot. This suited me fine, as I didn't want anyone to discover I was not much of a dribbler.

The highlight of being on the basketball team, as with all sports, was the bus ride to away games. The track bus was infinitely raunchier than the basketball bus. The basketball team consisted of girls who were less interested in boys, so we concentrated on being ridiculous as opposed to being naughty. We once had a contest to see whose legs could get the hairiest in a determined amount of time. Winna Arroyo won, and her leg display was quite pretty because she's a redhead. A few of us even held a nipple-hair challenge. I didn't win that one, happily. We sang commercial jingles, had potato chip and tootsie roll fights, held arm, leg, and thumb-wrestling contests, taped our faces into ugly contortions with medical tape, and rubbed Ben-Gay under the noses of anyone who fell asleep. We barely cared about the game we were headed to or had just come from. We saved the worrying for the court.

The gyms of Aspen, Meeker, Rangeley, Hayden, Craig, Rifle, and Vail (who called their team Roaring Fork) were much the same as our gym at home. Cinderblock walls and a shiny, wood floor with only enough room in the pull-out wooden bleachers for a few hundred people. These gyms were old enough to have absorbed the smells of 30 years or more of basketball rubber, sweat, and floor-wax, and when you walked into them empty, they almost seemed to echo the sounds of championship games of days gone by, or coaches hollering at practice. Each one reminded me of nights when I was little, when Dad would play in the city league, and we kids would chase each other under the bleachers and wait eagerly for half-time when we could run around on the court floor.

The team I played on won about half the time. I don't remember being incredibly upset or overjoyed with winning or losing. Girl's basketball at the time never attracted anyone more than our families and a few stray perverts, so without a cheering section it was not much more exhilarating than scrimmaging against ourselves. I do remember that the Roaring Fork girls were ruthless under the basket. We often walked away with scratches, bruises, and torn clothing—perhaps normal in boy's basketball, but unheard of in girl's—and a few times they offered to meet us outside after the game, where they would "hurt us." We didn't oblige, and didn't care if our honor was tarnished. We weren't men (or stupid) after all.

I had one perfect moment in my years as a basketball player—a glorious, overpowering, spiritual moment. It happened at a home game, with Dad yelling from the bleachers as usual. It started with a terrifying experience. I had somehow wandered out of my safe, hidden, center position to almost half court when someone passed me the ball. There was no one open to pass to, and malicious enemy team players were advancing toward me with their ball-stealing skills. I experienced a flash of panic, which inexplicably disappeared immediately and was replaced by a meditative calm. I looked at the basket as if in a silent dream, as if all the other players and sounds had disappeared and that lone basket was the only thing that existed. Against all my usual fears, I started dribbling. How this happened, I still don't know, but I started dribbling and moving forward and switching hands as each player came at me for the ball. I didn't think of passing; I headed on an obstacle course of sweaty girls straight for the basket. In and out, between and around people I proceeded until I was several feet to the right of the basket. From there my body mysteriously began to shoot the hardest shot of all—the hook. My right arm rounded over my head and let that bad boy fly right into the net with a swoosh. Before I could comprehend what happened, girls were jumping all over me, screaming and patting my back. I could hear my Dad hollering himself hoarse from the bleachers. I was laughing and smiling, and wondering what happened. The ref even patted my shoulder.

Unfortunately the game was not over, and we had to continue playing right after my shining moment. I was so dazed I could barely concentrate and probably played a pretty shitty game after that. But I am now a true believer in once-in-a-lifetime magical moments of superhuman feats.

Our girl's team never won any major tournaments while I was in high-school. We did well, and had more than our share of laughs, which could be considered a fantastic success if you're looking at life properly. My siblings ended up being closer to star material than I was. Debi made first five in the All-State Basketball tournament, and even got a scholarship to Regis College in Denver, and then transferred to Mesa College in Grand Junction on scholarship. Derick made first team All-State, first team All-State Tournament, and honorable mention All-State. (Not sure what all that means, but it's a lot of titles.) Like Debi, he won a scholarship to Mesa College and attended for a while, but transferred to San Diego State as a walk-on.

Today I miss playing basketball as a team. I shoot baskets by myself a couple days a week at my local gym, but I miss the camaraderie, teamwork, and heavy workout of playing on a team. Every now and then I'll walk by a gym and hear the squeak of tennis shoes, the drumming of the ball on the court, the rattle of the ball hitting the backboard, the shouting, the whistle. I'll smell sweat, and I'll wish I could run out there and get sweaty, too, and find one more of those magical superhuman moments.

Buses Unplugged

Our walk to the bus stop at the end of Huckleberry Lane was about a half of a mile. Because the dates of our school year were from September to late May, we were guaranteed nothing but cold temperatures to contend with on our stroll to catch the bus. To a kid who—at 7:30 in the morning—would rather be in bed anyway, the sometimes brutal cold seemed like punishment beyond reason.

When the temperature was above zero, we could make the best of it and pretend like we were having recess at school—chasing each other, throwing snowballs, occasionally dunking one another in the snow, sliding on our boots, butts, or books. Below zero we were common sufferers huddled together in a circle, stomping our boots, and banging our mittens together. At negative 30 and below our faces resembled those National Geographic photos of Antarctic trekkers with snowballs on their eyelashes and white beards. We would gawk at each other's frozen facial hair and talk about how strange it felt to have your nose hairs freeze your nostrils shut. All we did then was stare down the road looking for that bus.

Through the many years of my bus riding to Steamboat public schools we had two bus drivers. The first was Mr. Olsen, a blond hippie who must have been stoned all of the time. (It wouldn't have occurred to me back then but it seems obvious now.) He barely ever spoke to any of us kids, was droopy-eyed and slow, and let us wreak havoc. I suppose we followed the KEEP HEAD HANDS AND FEET INSIDE THE BUS rule, but he allowed screaming, fighting, bouncing from seat to seat, beating up on small children, cussing, throwing books and pencils, strangling the person in the seat in front of you, crawling under seats to avoid being strangled by the person behind you, loud music from transistor radios, crazy dancing to loud music, and (once that I remember) gluing someone else's pant legs together. There was lots of giving and receiving of noogies and wedgies. Hair-pulling was popular, and a few times Alan Tuck was de-panted by Jeff Fry. Although he allowed us to have our half-hour of "Lord of the Flies," we never really liked him. He didn't smile, for one thing. And we didn't know it at the time, but an adult who sets boundaries earns respect. The kids know the adult cares about them. We knew he didn't care about us, and we knew nothing about him except that he liked to party at the Tugboat, our local rowdy saloon, in the evenings.

Betsy Zimmerman was different. She took over the Fish Creek route when I was in early junior high. At first we were all mortified that a new driver might spoil the autonomy of our morning and afternoon lunatic asylum. We were suspicious of her marvelously friendly smile and whispered that we might be able to get rid of her if we were bad enough. It didn't take long to realize we were not the boss of Betsy. Her smile could turn quickly and efficiently to a stern and confident straight line. She wasn't afraid to kick troublemakers off the bus and make them walk. She never lost her temper, but she could get as determined and stubborn as the brattiest kid on the bus. It was literally her way or the highway. We learned to love her.

Every morning as we stomped snow off our boots and climbed onto the bus, she'd greet us with a smile. "How are you? Hey, it got above zero yesterday afternoon; think we might get it again today? Did you pass your French test yesterday?" Conversation?! She remembered my stupid test?! Nobody's *parents* even talked to them like that!

As we drove to pick up more kids, she was jovial and would talk to all of us from the front of the bus. She thought we were funny; she was always laughing. The kindergarteners and first-graders sat in the front seats of the bus, and Betsy had an endearing way of speaking to them. They were like frightened little bunnies after the chaos of the Mr. Olsen era, and they stayed as close to the door as they could. We could see from the reflection of Betsy's face in the big mirror at the front of the bus that she loved her little bunnies, and they were wide-eyed and giggly in return.

Every once in a while a kid would act up. Betsy would stop the bus, walk back to their seat with her straight-line mouth and say a few quiet words. The kid-in-question would be silent the rest of the trip, and the rest of us would be on our best behavior. We had thought that we had it made with Mr. Olsen's no-holds-barred policy, but life on the bus with Betsy was wonderful in comparison. We had an adult who cared.

The most famous of all Steamboat school bus drivers was Gonk. To this day people relay tales of his legendary exploits. He was known for his perfect black handlebar moustache and for driving fast. He was an ex-racecar driver. He could get us to Denver in two hours and 45 minutes, a time I've never been able to match before or since in any automobile. I've never heard of anyone else doing it, either, and he did it with a long bus full of kids.

I didn't ride Gonk's usual school route. I got him only for sports trips. We'd be happy to see him because it meant the trip would go fast. Sitting in the back of the bus held an extra bonus when Gonk drove. The physics of going around a corner at high speeds meant that back-seat riders would get thrown from one side of the bus to the other. We played it up a bit.

Few students liked to be at the front with Gonk. He drove so fast it was frightening. I tried it once, for the sport of it, but ended up skulking back and squeezing in with someone in the middle seats after an hour of white-knuckled clasping on the seat in front of me, certain we were going to die in a fiery crash at any moment. I think he loved speed, and might have gotten a little extra adrenaline buzz from racing like that with 77 live children in his care. I know some parents complained, but it wasn't enough to stop Gonk. He drove buses for an awfully long time.

Many years after I left Steamboat, I heard that Gonk had been fired for driving a school bus like a racecar. It seemed a good way for Gonk to go.

My mom drove a school bus, but not the Fish Creek Falls bus that we took. Her neighborhood was Fish Creek Meadows; she took the job for the extra money, and ended up doing it for eleven years.

Almost immediately Mom earned a respectable reputation at her post. She started the job with a busload of regular kids and one teenage terrorist. A kid who had just moved to Steamboat from Back East (in other words: an outsider, a city-slicker, a flat-lander, a hippie, a ski-bum) began his terror campaign on Mom's bus each morning before school. Mom said he was just plain bad, and his crimes were almost exclusively relegated to harming young children. Each morning an innocent child would end up in tears. Mom tried every threatening technique she knew of, and nothing intimidated the bad boy. Mom would come home angry, shouting, fed-up, and wondering why she'd ever taken on this impossible job. After two weeks of hell Mom got serious. With a busload of kids, she stopped her bus in front of the Superintendent's building. In front of all the kids she walked to back of the bus, grabbed the kid by the collar and dragged him off the bus. She hauled him into the building and threw him down onto a chair in the secretary's office where she was told that Mr. Sauer, the meanest superintendent in Christendom, would see the kid in a moment. Mom left in a huff, but was a little worried that she'd been wimpy and shirked her disciplinary duties by handing over her responsibility to someone higher up. An hour later she got a call that the kid had pulled a knife on Mr. Sauer.

The incident prompted the establishment of a new precedence in school bus policy; riding the bus was a privilege, not a right, and bad kids were kicked off for good. Mom had earned a level of respect from the community: she had not the slightest trouble with rowdy kids after they'd witnessed her dragging a kid by the scruff of his neck, she was deemed a worthy co-worker by the other bus drivers who considered the episode a decent rite of initiation, and the school board had no doubts that she was up to the job.

When Mom would return home from her route we'd hear stories every day of kids who were funny, kids she liked, bus-driver politics, mechanical troubles, or bad weather complaints. I loved hearing about it all. It served as decent gossip, and Mom has a glorious way of telling stories. With a straight face and a sincere belief that she's simply relaying facts, she puts a hilarious spin on any tale she tells. While the listener is rolling on the floor with tears squirting out of their eyes, she looks half-surprised that someone is listening to her, let alone being entertained.

There was nothing funny about driving the bus in bad weather. Steamboat can have some of the worst snowy weather conditions in the continental United States. We never got out of school due to snow; buses ran no matter what.

Once in a while buses had to go the route with a snowplow escort. In a whiteout blizzard the plow was necessary to clear a path in front of the bus. If the bus didn't drive right behind the plow the road would blow closed immediately after the plow passed through. Visibility was zero, and the flashing lights of the plow were a faint beacon to follow through the storm. Both vehicles could drive no faster than five miles-per-hour, and the kids would always be late for school, or late getting home. Sometimes the kids who lived out 20-Mile Road wouldn't get to school until 10 o'clock. No one envied the late kids on bad snow days. Bus drivers didn't allow one tiny sound from the kids in those conditions, and the high anxiety of the drivers most certainly rubbed off on the kids. On those days Betsy did not smile; she looked worried sick. Mom came home looking as if someone had bludgeoned her with a snow shovel.

Another problem that caused us to be late was that occasionally some prankster would unplug the buses. In cold places vehicles come equipped with electric engine heaters which should be plugged in at night when subzero temperatures are forecasted. In winter a lengthy cord was suspended above the long line of parked school buses; each bus was plugged into it. Rarely would someone be tough or crazy enough to brave the super-frozen temperatures and unplug them, but it did happen, and many of the buses wouldn't start without help from the bus mechanics. On those days we stood at our bus stop staring down the white road with our frozen breath and white eyebrows.

"Someone must have unplugged the buses," a kid would offer.

"Yep," we'd all agree.

There was little more to say. We may have been inconvenienced, but there were few children (or adults) who would disagree that it was a dreadfully good practical joke.

Icy roads also posed great dangers for the school buses. Our bus stop at the end of Huckleberry Lane met up with Fish Creek Falls Road as it ascended a hill. The city street crews would deposit a generous spray of gravel at the intersection to give something for drivers' wheels to grab onto while turning, slowing, or trying to get up the hill. They did not always make it to the spot before Betsy.

Of course icy-road-days were cold, and we kids would huddle together quietly watching for Betsy's yellow flashing lights to appear over the rise of the hill in the distance. When finally we saw our beacon we would sigh with relief and begin squirming and chattering like baby birds who see their mother coming with a mouthful of chewed-up worms. Betsy knew how oblivious we were to the perils of ice-driving, and began honking like a maniac as far as 500 yards away from our stop. We never took the clue that she would not be able to stop on the ice and get going up the hill afterward. Instead of stopping her plan was to pick up speed and fly through our stop, then pick us up later on the return trip. We pressed together, scrapping for the place that would get us on the bus first, getting more keyed up with every foot closer the bus approached. We would practically be out in the middle of the road with all our pushing and shoving. By the time the bus was close enough for us to see Betsy's face we knew we were in trouble. It was the only time Betsy looked crazy and mean. She would holler and honk and wave her arms for us to get the hell out of the way. We would scurry away as the bus roared past, and she would shake her fist at us and look at us like we were insane. Our hearts would sink into the depths of despair. The end of the route was another 15 minutes up the road. It would be a half hour before we were saved from freezing to death. We thought Betsy was the meanest woman in the world at those moments.

No matter how many times we got passed on icy days we never quit hoping that we'd get picked up. We'd wait too close to the road, sticking our saddest, most suffering eyes out as far as we could. Betsy would honk and holler as she passed, and scold us when we got on the bus a half hour later. We never learned. Being that cold just froze our brains and our memories.

The school bus became un-cool as we inched into our teenage years, and occasionally my friend Katie Lee and I would ski to school. Our neighborhood at Fish Creek was a couple miles up the mountain behind the high school, and from my house we could ski straight there. In a few places we'd have to glide as if on cross-country skis, but most of it was downhill.

It was quite surrealistic to experience the pure joy of flying free through the snow and trees and crisp air while on our way to our humdrum routine life. Katie and I would holler as we passed the few houses on the way, hoping to wake someone. We did a lot of screaming and laughing and knocking each other over. We'd show up for school wet or snow-covered, tromping in our ski boots with our skis over our shoulders. No one paid much attention. Minutes after we'd just bonded with nature, had a good round of primal scream therapy, and had some of the world's best recreation, we were in our wooden desks writing Algebra problems.

One reason I didn't do it more often was because we had to dress like Eskimos, and I was too lazy to dress and undress in all that over-wear. In addition there was the issue of ski-equipment. We'd have to make arrangements to put it somewhere while at school, and then haul it on the bus home. (Betsy was happy to accommodate us.) Now that I look back it seems like a tiny price to pay for an experience many people would fly across the globe and pay thousands of dollars for.

Another reason we didn't ski everyday was the lure of blasting heaters on the bus. Glamorous or not, skiing could rarely hold a candle to the experience of sitting anywhere that was 90 degrees. Betsy would have the heaters cranked to full blast; nothing could be more inviting than 40 mile-per-hour scorching hot wind being blown over you when you felt like a popsicle.

Besides being un-cool, the school bus lost its pizzazz by the time we reached late high school. We loved Betsy, but after years of hearing screaming kids for an hour a day we'd had our fill. We were too old to participate in Recess on Wheels, and we'd given up on talking to each other over the din. Katie, Jill Wood, and I would stare out the window like zombies and watch the aspens go by. Our reign as kings of the coach was gladly turned over to our successors whose antics were far inferior to ours, we thought. Less inventive, less mean-spirited, not nearly as finely tuned. We carried our evil bus activities to a much more sophisticated arena—sports trips.

        The nearest towns to Steamboat that were available to compete at sports were quite a drive away. Craig was one hour, Meeker and Rifle were two, and Rangeley was three. Sometimes we'd compete against Aspen which was over four hours away. These long trips afforded ample opportunity to cause trouble, and the worst of us hell-raisers sat at the back of the bus. Although we were mildly mischievous on the basketball bus, my girlfriends and I made the biggest nuisance on trips to track meets.

        Our most frequent pastime was singing lovely melodies with the raunchiest lyrics we could possible make up. It would be impossible to print them here, but I will say with assuredness that a locker room full of men would have a hard time coming up with worse. These songs separated the women from the girls, so to speak. The songs were so obscene that several of the singers eventually gave up with disgust and permanently moved to the middle of the bus. It was understood that the faint-of-heart would not be able to endure the vulgarity of the last three rows of seats, and the bad-girl club became rather select. I'm sure the good-girls didn't care one iota about missing out.

        When we'd tire of dirty songs, someone would crank the boom-box. To the blaring roar of Van Halen, AC/DC,

Foreigner, REO Speedwagon, or Cheap Trick, we'd sing, play air guitar, and do mock strip teases. Ruthless gossip was a must, and once in a while a girl would sneak a Playgirl on the bus (which we laughed at, but thought was disgusting). We'd do nasty imitations of nerdy girls at school or movie stars of all kinds. (Melanie Sprengle did an excellent Incredible Hulk impersonation.)

Only once did we get in serious trouble for our antics. We were driving though Craig, an agrarian town stuck in the 1950s, and on cue pulled our pants down and mooned its citizens from every window. Our coach, Franny, screamed, "LADIES!" and stomped down the aisles shouting at us, absolutely appalled. Betsy, who sometimes drove the bus for track trips, was mortified and stopped the bus for a steaming lecture. We listened and shut-up, but were mystified. What was so bad about mooning Craig? We considered the other things we did on the bus a hundred times more crude. It didn't occur to us that showing our bare butts from a vehicle that carried the words Steamboat Springs Public School District was a problem.

We endeavored to be the very naughtiest we could, but it was all talk. We were all virgins, got good grades, were some of the best athletes in school, and wouldn't touch drugs, or, very rarely, as noted, alcohol. A pinch between the cheek and gum of Copenhagen or Skoal was as far as we ventured into the world of forbidden substance use, and that was only for special occasions. Our wicked antics were a mandatory and probably even healthy outlet for girls who were obedient to ample discipline at home and school, and had blossoming hormones and curiosity galore.

On trips back home from a long day of track events, with a fist full of ribbons and trophies, we'd stuff our faces with candy bars, cake, and pop. As the sun set we'd start singing, "Oh she looked so fair in the midnight air as the wind blew up her…" In the dark we'd tell gross stories with a flashlight in our face until eventually we'd nod off one by one with our heads on each other's shoulders, and no one could tell us from the goody-two-shoes girls in the middle of the bus.

My Steamboat

Months after graduating from high school I left Steamboat with lofty dreams of making my splash in the world. The day before I moved away I sat on a rock by the New House overlooking the town, the Yampa Valley, the mountain, and felt deep sadness. Dad had told us we would never see a place so beautiful, and I believed him.

I lived in Boulder, Colorado for ten years where I studied art at CU, and I got married. Then I traveled around the country on a fabulous motor-home adventure for the next three years, making and selling art, until I found the place I wanted to settle. I chose the South because it reminded me of how Steamboat was a long time ago: unpretentious, beautiful, and inexpensive. I have not missed the cold in the least, but I am the saddest girl in the world when I can't come home for that white Christmas. In the past few years I've remarried and started an art gallery that keeps me from traveling much; I don't get home to Steamboat near as often as I'd like to.

Soon after moving away from Steamboat at age 17, I found out, to my surprise, that my hometown was already quite well-known—a sought-after destination. (I don't know how this fact slipped my mind when I'd witnessed tourists and outsiders coming in droves every winter.) When new acquaintances would find out I was from Steamboat I'd see their eyes light up, and I'd hear, "Oh! You must be a good skier." Or "Wow. I've been there once. That place is beautiful." I had felt isolated from the larger world growing up, and I didn't have much to compare Steamboat to, so I figured my hometown was just like anyplace else. No big deal. Seeing that people were not only interested, they were jealous and intrigued by my status as a Steamboat native, I began to feel both proud and annoyed. It was fine that people were impressed by Steamboat, but sometimes I'd get sick of people trying to one-up me with their accounts of how many times they'd been there, how long they lived there, or who they knew with a condo there. They obviously could not comprehend that these "accomplishments" meant absolutely nothing to me. I didn't see the place the way they did. My grandparents had lived there since the 1940s. How could I see living in our quiet little town as a status symbol?

What awarded a person the status of "local" or "native" became cause for serious argument, one that I had no interest in. Once, at an exhibit of my paintings, long after I'd moved away from home, a man read in my bio that I was from Steamboat and said, "Yes, but are you *from* Steamboat?"

Having heard this comment a hundred times I replied amicably, "Well, I was born and raised there, but I don't live there any more." I hoped, in vain, that this would be the end of it.

"So, you're not really *from* there."

I sighed. Not this again. "Depends on what you mean by from, I guess. I don't live there now."

"OK. So you're not *from* there."

I wanted to tell him to get a life, but I said, nicely as always, "I guess not."

He promptly went on to tell me how he and his wife have spent the past 20 winters there, in their fancy condo, and did I know the Reisners? Oh, of course I didn't because I wasn't FROM there.

My family still has to put up with this debate in Steamboat, and they still pay no attention to those vying for local status.

Grampa was 91 when he died last summer. I went home for the funeral. I hadn't been home in two and half years—the longest stretch ever. I didn't know what to expect.

I flew into Denver so that I could rent a car and experience the three-hour drive through the mountains. In summer the journey is spectacular and a million times safer than winter; I know every turn and view along the way from my countless crossings during college. Much of the trip was the same as I remembered it, except that the traffic on the roads has increased tenfold (or more), some terrible beetle blight has turned many of the pine-covered mountain peaks to rusty brown, and the little town of Silverthorne— where there used to be nothing but a dirty gas station for our half-way stop on the way to and from Denver—is now a tumultuous commercial extravaganza with condos and gargantuan log homes and chain stores and 188 outlet stores and traffic as crazy as New York City. I moved right on through.

As I rounded the last bend on Rabbit Ears to take me down into the Yampa Valley, I saw Steamboat nestled in the distance like it always was. I somehow expected it might look different—bigger or shinier or something—but it was the same. A sense of exhilaration and apprehension came over me as I got closer to town. I was excited to be home, but worried that the changes would be overwhelming. I was afraid it would be so different that I would feel no sense of familiarity, that I would be an outsider, that my beautiful hometown would belong to someone else now.

I did see that some quiet farms and fields had been replaced with strip malls and parking lots. I saw plenty of traffic and gobs of tourists walking around on Main Street. The storefronts get fancier every time I go home; the town looks like a colorful, polished replica of an old ranch town instead of an old ranch town. But a good omen came to me a few minutes after I drove in. Directing traffic at a broken streetlight was policeman Shane Jacobs (son of Gonk Jacobs, the bus driver, and brother of Judd Jacobs who smooched Jeanette Green under the slide). Shane was in my class from kindergarten through twelfth grade. Grownup Shane didn't notice me, but I was smiling ear to ear just to see him.

I had decided to stay with Derick while in town. I have quite a few accommodations to choose from when I go home. Dana still lives there, and Mom and Dad divorced long ago, so I can stay with either of them. They split up at the end of my high school years; although my parents easily agreed on being thrifty and on how to raise kids and animals, their interests and personalities were so different it's a wonder they stayed together as long as they did.

I pulled up to Derick's luxurious home exhausted from the many hours of traveling, so I took a long nap. For the most part, we kids did not follow in the footsteps of our thrifty parents. In fact, it's not uncommon for us to be downright extravagant. Whether we have a lot of money or not, I think we had our fill of Trading Post mentality.

I woke in time to go see Derick's softball game at the same Howelson ball field where we all played as kids. It felt mighty interesting sitting on those same metal bleachers yelling "Go Derick" through that same chain link fence. Just like always, the temperature dropped 20 degrees after the sun went down, and I knew enough to bring along a blanket. My sister Dana and I snuggled under it just like 30 years ago and yelled "Go Derick" together.

Grampa's funeral took place the next morning. I was nervous. At 42, I'd never been to a funeral before! Derick, his wife Anne, and I walked into Holy Name Catholic Church entryway and were greeted by a good crowd of Duckels relatives, some of whom I did not know but bore an incredible resemblance to Granny. No one seemed sad; everyone was happy to see each other. We shook hands and hugged and smiled and stood next to each other. When it was time to go into the chapel I smiled as I dipped my hand into holy water, suppressing my urge to flick someone. I sat in the sixth row from the front on the left side with Anne.

The church looked so much smaller than I remembered it. I now attend church in a grand, city cathedral (where I drift off into Catholic Land just like Dad used to) and the church of my upbringing seems like a little country chapel in comparison. I used to think the wooden beams of Holy Name were towering buttresses that reached to the sky. I was baptized, had my first communion, was confirmed, and married (the first time) at Holy Name, and now, my first funeral. I'll get no closer to fulfilling all the sacraments until I'm on my deathbed.

Grampa's coffin was placed in the center aisle. Due
to my inexperience with funerals I found myself surprised to
realize that Grampa was there, in that coffin, in this church,
with us right then. Most of my family stood in the pews in
front of us. I recognized many of the people attending the
service from the days of going to church with Dad. I looked
around at the church itself and remembered that Grampa
and company had long ago erected those beautiful wood
beams that supported it.

I would not have guessed that I would have become
so emotional. That church so full of memories, those people
I'd not seen in so long. Instead of grief I was overcome with a
sense of gratitude, hope, and compassion, and I certainly
couldn't say why. Maybe many people feel this way at a
funeral.

My cousin Chuckie was the first to speak about
Grampa. (He goes by Chuck now, but I can't think of him as
anyone other than Chuckie.) His speech was most interesting
and completely shocking to me. He focused on the genealogy
of Grampa's side of the family. Until this speech I had
believed what Grampa had once told me about his family.

"Where do we come from, Grampa? Who are our
people?"

"Oh, we used to be in England, but you won't find a
Duckels there any more. We were bad. We were all shot or
hung or run out."

That was the end of it. The only thing I'd ever heard
about our people.

Apparently Chuckie has been researching our roots
for over a decade, and came up with all sorts of information
to discount what Grampa had told me. He'd come up with
proof that we were related to all sorts of famous and
respectable historical figures all the way back to the

Jamestown settlement. I wasn't sure if genealogy reports were the norm at funerals, but I was immensely pleased that I got to hear it. For all those years I thought my family descended from a horde of ruffians and ne'er-do-wells. I don't know why it makes a difference to know that your ancestors amounted to something, but it did to me. Suddenly, instead of descending from rotten stock, I was related to most everyone in America. Just like when I realized I wasn't the Ugliest Girl in the World, my world opened a little.

My Dad spoke about Grampa in a way Grampa would have spoken about someone he loved. Dad told stories. Simple, honest, funny stories. He spoke with pride about Grampa's unpretentiousness, strength, and tenacity—all qualities Dad tried to pass on to me. Dad's manner, as usual, was quiet and to the point. It's always a treat to get to hear him speak. Out loud. Tears rolled down my cheeks, and Anne passed me Kleenex.

I have no funerals to compare it with, but I thought the service was lovely. I was overjoyed that the priest went through the full mass. I recited my responses with gusto, just like Debi and I used to. I was very disappointed to see that the altar boy no longer rang a bell at all when the priest raised his chalice.

After the service we all drove in a long line behind a police car to our favorite place—the graveyard. I couldn't admit to anyone how much I anticipated going up there again. As we drove up the hill I hoped that it hadn't changed, and much to my relief it had not. It was still small and modest.

Grampa's gravesite was next to the Webber's, whose epitaph has an engraving of our beloved Roving Christmas Tree, the tradition they had started. Grampa's gravestone will look nice next to theirs; Granny has ordered engravings of praying hands, a cross, and a big bulldozer.

As we listened to the short service the burning high-altitude sun beat down on us in our black outfits. Granny was given a flag in honor of Grampa's military service, the priest tossed dirt on the coffin and said the same things they say on TV funerals. It was fascinating to witness it for the first time in real life. We were all told to go to Dad's house for a reception afterwards, and as Derick, Dana, Anne and I drove out of the place I begged Derick to drive slowly so we could shout out the names of people we knew. We did. There were plenty more graves than years before, but few with names that I did not recognize.

Dad's house is one the most fabulous places on Earth, and I mean it. It's bordered on four sides by National Forest, has a roaring creek running next to it, and looks like Ralph Lauren decorated it personally. The setting, along with the splendid feast laid out by Sunny, my stepmom, made for a reception that could have been featured in Martha Stewart Living magazine. After my parent's divorce and before he met Sunny, Dad stayed true to his simple, Spartan tastes and needed no more than a roof over his head, a chair, a TV, and a newspaper to satisfy his needs. Sunny livened up his life with fine comforts, and I am quite sure he enjoys it. I marveled at how things had changed for Dad since the days of carving up deer carcasses in the kitchen.

I pumped cousin Chuckie for more info about our roots, ate too many chocolate bar thingys, caught up with relatives I haven't seen since I was tiny, and shared my favorite quotes from Grampa.

I spent the next day with my Mom. The two-mile drive up Fish Creek Falls Road, which was once lonely and quiet, is completely, totally, 100 percent lined with homes. The hill on which Katie and I skied to school is a crowded subdivision from top to bottom.

Mom still lives in the New House, which of course isn't new anymore. It seemed big when we first lived there, but the average house today is three times the size. The simple exterior fit in when we built the house in the early 70's, but has long outlived the trends of that time. Mom's interior décor is still a feast for the eye. She's got the groovy trinkets from my childhood, Baroque antiques she inherited from Ahvee, and garage sale treasures picked up through the years. I spent the first ten minutes there scanning all her stuff and remembering half my life. Her breathtaking view of town is gone; a subdivision of three-story homes took that away a few years ago. Another bunch of homes blocks the front of the house from the potential walk-to-Canada-without-seeing-humanity.

As always with Mom we talked about our lives, relationships, art and writing, God, and ever-changing Steamboat. And of course I needed to be caught up on local news. Mom has changed in some ways since my younger days. She is still outspoken, independent, and artsy, but has cleaned up her language and softened her manner. She has always been unswervingly supportive of my endeavors at everything; I always feel like I could conquer the world after I've been with her.

She no longer tosses cats. In fact, cats are now her cherished companions. They come indoors when it's cold, and are pampered like mini-humans. She even spends hundreds of dollars on veterinarian bills!

She told me she's subdividing her property into tiny lots. The land she and Dad bought for $200 an acre now sells for hundreds of thousands for an eighth of an acre. She is the last holdout on the mountain to succumb to developers. This means that eventually all her land will be covered with big log homes crammed together, and will match perfectly all the surrounding big log homes crammed together. This is the four acres of aspen groves, sagebrush, and grasses that Casey grazed upon, where we picked Columbines when we weren't supposed to, where we made hula skirts out of the skunk cabbage, and did woodland skits for the neighbors. So many snowmen and sledding hills were built upon this land you could never count them. But I understand. Like many of the old-timers in Steamboat (and other pastoral-towns-turned-mega-tourist-resorts) Mom can barely afford the outrageously high taxes on her property that she's owned in full for decades. It's difficult for ranchers and landowners who are barely scraping by to turn down the mass sums of money waved at them by developers. It's surprising that more idyllic pastures haven't turned to asphalt or vacation homes for the wealthy.

A few years ago, I attended a party in Steamboat with Dad and Sunny. At a palatial log home (sounds like an oxymoron, but no, not anymore) I was chatting with a woman from Virginia Beach who had recently purchased a vacation home in Steamboat. She seemed like a nice woman until she brought up the subject of the new low-income housing apartments that were then being planned for Steamboat.

"People should have to earn the right to live here," she said with disgust.

My smiling face fell. Who did she think worked in the restaurants and hotels? More and more employed people, especially in the service industry, had to move to towns such as Hayden and Craig to find affordable housing. They commute up to an hour for a low-paying job. Many of the people I grew up with, Steamboat *natives*, holders of the most sought-after title in town, can't afford much more than those inexpensive apartments. They've lived in Steamboat their entire lives, yet, according to this woman, don't deserve to live there. I was so mad I knew I'd better not get started, so I didn't. I found the quickest opportunity to gracefully excuse myself and left her to eat her braised artichoke appetizer by herself.

Mom and I went for a glorious walk at the relatively new Yampa Botanical Gardens and had a treat at one of the six local Starbucks. Although Steamboat fought for years to keep the chain stores away, they eventually yielded in a big way. It's hard not to give in to big-city expedience and made-in-China prices. Although something sacred is lost when Wal-Mart and McDonald's comes to town, I know how inconvenient it can be to live three and half hours away (or more in winter) from the nearest clothes you can afford.

We tried to eat lunch at a cutesy restaurant, but after a difficult search for a parking space we were turned away by an hour-and-a-half waiting list! This is the town that used to practically shut down in the offseason—where one was lucky to find even a single person eating in a restaurant in the summer. Now traffic putts down Main Street day and night, year round.

Mom knew of a casual place west of town. We were relieved to find plenty of tables open for us, and every person eating there looked as informal and unassuming as the people I grew up with.

"Everyone here is a native, huh, Mom?"

Mom looked around. "Looks like it. It's funny how you can tell."

Dana and her boyfriend, Mark, joined us at the restaurant after a bit and we spent the afternoon giggling. I often wish I could be more like Dana. She is the youngest and has that youngest-child carefree outlook that I could use more of. I asked her how she handles all the changes in Steamboat. She said she chooses to stay in denial. "If I thought about it I'd have to move, so I don't think about it."

Derick invited Mom and Dana over for a small gathering at his home that evening. We laughed our heads off most of the time, telling our worn-out family stories to Mark, Dana's boyfriend, who might have been overwhelmed by our rowdiness. Debi is the funniest of us all, and had she been there we would have really scared Mark with our noise. She now owns her own successful construction consulting company in Florida, but unfortunately couldn't make the trip due to illness. We had pizza by the backyard waterfall, and I beamed when Derick went through a ton of trouble to light his twenty state-of-the-art tiki torches just for us. Then we watched a movie on his super-gigantic-flat-screen-high-definition-TV with seven surround-sound speakers. We made him play certain loud scenes over and over so we could feel the house rumble.

My siblings and I have all turned out to live very different lives, but getting together is usually the same. No matter how our lives differ we still carry a similar outlook on things. We all find it easy to see the odd and comical in everything. Both parents taught us that to be phony is a horrific sin, and, for better or worse, our personalities are blatantly apparent for the world to see. Although we don't deny our pain when we have it, we all have a steadfast optimism and enjoy sharing it when we're together. Like most families, we have had stretches where some of us didn't get along, but so far we've found that things patch themselves up eventually.

I kept the following morning open to spend time with Dad. Big surprise! He wanted to go for a ride. He needed to check out his construction sites, and I was more than happy to go with him. Now 70 years old, he still works as hard as ever (almost never a day off) but his company is large now so he does a lot of bossing people around, mostly.

I don't know what I expected to be different about going for a ride with Dad, but I assumed something might have changed. It had not. I got in a diesel pick-up truck (one of many in his company fleet) that smelled of mechanic's grease and bologna sandwiches. I had to move a few pop cans to the floor and wipe some dirt off the seat. I knew better than to ask where we were going or how long we'd be gone. I knew we'd just wander around town and take how long we took. Dad drove at his usual easygoing pace, sometimes humming Christmas tunes, sometimes quiet.

We stopped first at his gravel pit where he explained in minute detail how the crusher worked. I did not ask him to; this is what he always does. At some point in my life he's explained exactly how each and every kind of construction equipment works. He encourages questions and gives clear, well-defined answers to make sure you understand. Surrounding the explanation are stories of successes and failures of that particular piece of equipment, accounts of employees who have harmed or been harmed by the machine, and where he got it and how much he paid for it. For Dad this ritual is as sacred as anything he recites in church. I watched him closely and asked lots of questions (because it really is interesting) and saw his eyes sparkle with pride and enthusiasm.

We left the pit and took 20 Mile Road into town. Dad told me some stories about old Steamboat as I looked out at the golden fields and small ranches. We ducked through town to see his bridge job on Soda Creek (right where we got drunk in the Willys Jeep for Christmas caroling) and then up Fish Creek and over to the golf course. We checked out a subdivision he built that now sports castle-size log homes that billionaires use for a few weeks out of the year. Then we went out Highway 131—the bottomland of the Yampa Valley, featured in outdoor magazines and calendar covers— to Stagecoach, where he's building a new subdivision. I asked him long ago how he felt about plowing down the beautiful countryside he's always loved. He said he didn't exactly like all the changes and growth, but he's not the one who decides what's going to be built where. That's up to developers. Someone is going to do the construction work, and since it's his job, that's what he does. His viewpoint is much like the farmers and ranchers around the area. They don't complain as much as you'd think about the transformation of the region; they are so close to the land and the seasons they know better than anyone how to accept change and about our inability to control things.

For four hours I was comforted by the purring of his diesel truck and the quiet, familiar sound of that man's voice. I watched the crisp shadow of the pick-up floating over wildflowers by the side of the road, and found myself trying to spot elk and deer on the ridges, like Dad had taught me. I blurred my eyes as we drove by aspen groves so the white trunks on the dark forest background looked like zebra stripes. I remembered the dreams I'd nursed while gazing at the passing hay bales and barbwire fences. When we drove slowly over the newly broken roads his company was building, his truck bumped and bounced us around, and I let my head be tossed about like Debi and I did when we played Monkey Business. It's not often that people get to go back and do something exactly and precisely the way they did it when they were small children. I was filled with gratitude that I did.

When we got back to the shop (the Duckels Construction compound) I got out of the pick-up to find a big smudge of black grease on my dress. I almost said shit, but decided no, this is perfect.

On my last morning in town I took a walk from Derick's house to the ranchland out near Sleeping Giant, the countryside that had always been my favorite in the area. Like all Steamboat mornings it was cool enough to need a jacket and long pants. Steel blue mountains in the distance rise above pastureland of yellow rustling wheat, and tall willows crowd the Elk River which runs through the valley. The land is broken into large ranches, so cattle and hay bales dot the area. I like it because it is the most peaceful place I've ever been. I walked on the dirt road and ran my hands across the top of the grasses and breathed in the strong smell of sage. I headed off the road, over a small rise on a hill, and found an old, rusted, 1940's Adams County Fire Truck. I remembered finding lost treasures abandoned in fields so many times in childhood; we would have climbed on the truck and pretended to be rushing off to some fire. In the back of the wooden flat bed was an enormous pile of discarded skis, all from the 1970s. I have no idea why they were there, but I wondered if, somewhere under the hundreds of Mark IVs, Rossignols and K2s, there was a pair of heavy, scratched, silver Spauldings rotting into oblivion.

People come from all over the world to visit a paradise like Steamboat. After being gone so long I had the same measure of awe and inspiration at the natural surroundings that a newcomer would have. But this was combined with my deep, cellular familiarity of a place that had shaped my whole being from birth. Since I arrived in town I experienced a dreamlike, back-and-forth swing between my fresh outlook and my entrenched connection, and although it was stirring, it was hard in a way. Melancholy would be the word to describe it.

I'd thought that the growth and change in me and in Steamboat might have made us an incompatible pair. My trip home showed me just the opposite. Although the face and pace of the town has changed quite dramatically, I still managed to spend my time very much like I used to. I found that it is still possible to overlook the tourists and go on with life, but benefit from the conveniences they bring. Thanks to the love of my family and the beauty of the Yampa Valley, I can still call the place "my Steamboat."

About the Author

Dori DeCamillis, a nationally-recognized visual artist, was born in Steamboat Springs, Colorado. In her late 20s she traveled the United States for three years in a vintage motor home, selling her paintings at outdoor art festivals. Her first book, "The Freeway," chronicles her hair-raising adventures on the road. DeCamillis owns Red Dot Gallery in Birmingham, Alabama. See her gallery, paintings, and books at www.reddotgallery.com.

Acknowledgements

Thank you very much to my early readers Anne LaPlante, Steve Dunlap, Rachel White, Susan Haynes, Chuck Solomon, Mary Kay Culpepper, and everyone in my family for input and encouragement.

Thanks a heap to Avery Hurt, my editor, for truly understanding the tone and imagery I meant to project, and for the honesty and tact to help me express it. Also for her superior use of the colon, which always seems to elude me. (The colon on the typewriter, not the other one.)

Thank you, thank you to Buddy Bair, the extraordinary photographer, whose vision and contagious enthusiasm produced the lovely photo for the front and back cover. Also thanks to Ivy and Aubrey Bair, Logan Sherar, and Katelynn Duckels for their excellent modeling job, and their parents for letting them do it. Thanks to Dad for building the bridge in the background of the shot. My sister Debi worked on it, she says.

Special thanks to Annabelle DeCamillis and Scott Bennett for always being there for me (and I mean always) and for cheering me on while I've worked my fanny off on writing, publishing, and selling this book.

Made in the USA
Lexington, KY
18 February 2011